U·X·L
Encyclopedia
of Science

U·X·L
Encyclopedia
of Science

Second Edition
Volume 6: H-Mar

Rob Nagel, Editor ■----------

GALE GROUP
THOMSON LEARNING

Detroit • New York • San Diego • San Francisco
Boston • New Haven, Conn. • Waterville, Maine
London • Munich

U·X·L
Encyclopedia of Science
Second Edition

Rob Nagel, *Editor*

Staff

Elizabeth Shaw Grunow, *U•X•L Editor*

Julie Carnagie, *Contributing Editor*

Carol DeKane Nagel, *U•X•L Managing Editor*

Thomas L. Romig, *U•X•L Publisher*

Shalice Shah-Caldwell, *Permissions Associate (Pictures)*

Robyn Young, *Imaging and Multimedia Content Editor*

Rita Wimberley, *Senior Buyer*

Pamela A. E. Galbreath, *Senior Art Designer*

Michelle Cadorée, *Indexing*

GGS Information Services, *Typesetting*

On the front cover: Nikola Tesla with one of his generators, reproduced by permission of the Granger Collection.

On the back cover: The flow of red blood cells through blood vessels, reproduced by permission of Phototake.

Library of Congress Cataloging-in-Publication Data

U-X-L encyclopedia of science.—2nd ed. / Rob Nagel, editor
  p.cm.
  Includes bibliographical references and indexes.
  Contents: v.1. A-As — v.2. At-Car — v.3. Cat-Cy — v.4. D-Em — v.5. En-G — v.6. H-Mar — v.7. Mas-O — v.8. P-Ra — v.9. Re-St — v.10. Su-Z.
  Summary: Includes 600 topics in the life, earth, and physical sciences as well as in engineering, technology, math, environmental science, and psychology.
  ISBN 0-7876-5432-9 (set : acid-free paper) — ISBN 0-7876-5433-7 (v.1 : acid-free paper) — ISBN 0-7876-5434-5 (v.2 : acid-free paper) — ISBN 0-7876-5435-3 (v.3 : acid-free paper) — ISBN 0-7876-5436-1 (v.4 : acid-free paper) — ISBN 0-7876-5437-X (v.5 : acid-free paper) — ISBN 0-7876-5438-8 (v.6 : acid-free paper) — ISBN 0-7876-5439-6 (v.7 : acid-free paper) — ISBN 0-7876-5440-X (v.8 : acid-free paper) — ISBN 0-7876-5441-8 (v.9 : acid-free paper) — ISBN 0-7876-5775-1 (v.10 : acid-free paper)

  1. Science-Encyclopedias, Juvenile. 2. Technology-Encyclopedias, Juvenile. [1. Science-Encyclopedias. 2. Technology-Encyclopedias.] I. Title: UXL encyclopedia of science. II. Nagel, Rob.
  Q121.U18 2001
  503-dc21
                                                                              2001035562

Printed in the United States of America

10 9 8 7 6 5 4 3 2 1

Table of Contents

Contents

Reader's Guide

Demystify scientific theories, controversies, discoveries, and phenomena with the *U•X•L Encyclopedia of Science,* Second Edition.

This alphabetically organized ten-volume set opens up the entire world of science in clear, nontechnical language. More than 600 entries—an increase of more than 10 percent from the first edition—provide fascinating facts covering the entire spectrum of science. This second edition features more than 50 new entries and more than 100 updated entries. These informative essays range from 250 to 2,500 words, many of which include helpful sidebar boxes that highlight fascinating facts and phenomena. Topics profiled are related to the physical, life, and earth sciences, as well as to math, psychology, engineering, technology, and the environment.

In addition to solid information, the *Encyclopedia* also provides these features:

- "Words to Know" boxes that define commonly used terms
- Extensive cross references that lead directly to related entries
- A table of contents by scientific field that organizes the entries
- More than 600 color and black-and-white photos and technical drawings
- Sources for further study, including books, magazines, and Web sites

Each volume concludes with a cumulative subject index, making it easy to locate quickly the theories, people, objects, and inventions discussed throughout the *U•X•L Encyclopedia of Science,* Second Edition.

Suggestions

We welcome any comments on this work and suggestions for entries to feature in future editions of *U•X•L Encyclopedia of Science*. Please write: Editors, *U•X•L Encyclopedia of Science,* U•X•L, Gale Group, 27500 Drake Road, Farmington Hills, Michigan, 48331-3535; call toll-free: 800-877-4253; fax to: 248-699-8097; or send an e-mail via www.galegroup.com.

Entries by Scientific Field

Boldface indicates volume numbers.

Entries by
Scientific Field

Atomic/Nuclear physics

Automotive engineering

Bacteriology

Ballistics

Biochemistry

Biology

Biomedical engineering

Biotechnology

Botany

Cartography

Electrical engineering

Electronics

Metallurgy

Meteorology

Microbiology

Mineralogy

Molecular biology

Technology

Half-life

Half-life is a measurement of the time it takes for one-half of a radioactive substance to decay (in this sense, decay does not mean to rot, but to diminish in quantity).

The atoms of radioactive substances, such as uranium and radium, spontaneously break down over time, transforming themselves into atoms of another element. In the process, they give off radiation, or energy emitted in the form of waves. An important feature of the radioactive decay process is that each substance decays at its own rate. The half-life of a particular substance, therefore, is constant and is not affected by any physical conditions (temperature, pressure, etc.) that occur around it.

Because of this stable process, scientists are able to estimate when a particular substance was formed by measuring the amount of original and transformed atoms in that substance. For example, the amount of carbon in a fossil sample can be measured to determine the age of that fossil. It is known that the radioactive substance carbon-14 has a half-life of 5,570 years. The half-lives of other radioactive substances can range from tiny fractions of a second to quadrillions of years.

[*See also* **Dating techniques; Geologic time; Isotope; Radioactivity**]

Hallucinogens

Hallucinogens are natural and human-made substances that often cause people to believe they see random colors, patterns, events, and objects

Words to Know

Hallucinations: Images, sounds, or odors that are seen, heard, or smelled by a person, but do not exist in reality.

Neurotransmitter: Chemical substance that transmits impulses between neurons (nerve cells) in the brain.

Synesthesia: A mixing of the senses so that one who experiences it claims to be able to taste color, or hear taste, or smell sounds.

that do not exist. The hallucinatory experiences can either be very pleasant or very disturbing. Many different types of substances are classified as hallucinogens because of their capacity to produce such hallucinations. These substances come in the form of pills, powders, liquids, gases, and plants that can be eaten. In the body, hallucinogens stimulate the nervous system. Effects include the dilation (widening) of the pupils of the eyes, constriction of certain arteries, and rising blood pressure.

Hallucinogens have long been a part of the religious rites of various cultures throughout history. Tribal shamen or medicine men swallowed the hallucinogenic substance or inhaled fumes or smoke from a burning substance to experience hallucinations. They believed that such a state enhanced their mystical powers. Separated from reality, they were better able to communicate with the gods or their ancestors. These hallucinogens were mostly natural substances. Among the oldest are those from mushrooms or cactus that have been used in Native American rites since before recorded time. The use of such compounds still forms a central part of tribal ritual in some Native American tribes.

Mushrooms

Certain species of mushrooms have been used for centuries by medicine men to bring about hallucinations. Although artifacts remaining from ancient cultures show mushrooms surrounded by human figures, the significance of such statues remained obscure for many years. Scientists were not aware of the existence of hallucinogenic mushrooms and their part in tribal rituals until the twentieth century.

After collecting and analyzing these mushrooms, scientists found that their active ingredient had a chemical structure similar to serotonin, a neurotransmitter in the brain. (A neurotransmitter is a chemical substance that transmits impulses between neurons [nerve cells] in the brain.) They named this ingredient psilocybin (pronounced sigh-luh-SIGH-ben).

In rituals, hallucinogenic mushrooms are either eaten directly or boiled in a liquid, which is then consumed. A user experiences enhanced colors and sounds, perceives objects or persons who are not present, and sometimes has terrifying visions that predict dire circumstances to come.

Peyote

Peyote is another ancient, natural hallucinogenic substance. It comes from the cactus species *Lophophora* that is native to the southwestern United States and Mexico. Peyote is the flowering mushroomlike head or button of the cactus. It contains a potent chemical substance called mescaline. Peyote is either chewed, boiled in a liquid for drinking, or rolled into pellets that are swallowed. The uses of peyote parallel those of the hallucinogenic mushrooms. Mescaline produces visions and changes in perception, and users experience a state of intoxication and happiness. Native Americans of the Southwest often use peyote in their tribal rituals. It is an especially important part of the Native American Church.

LSD

LSD (lysergic acid diethylamide; pronounced lie-SIR-jic A-sid die-ETH-a-la-mide) is a synthetic substance first made in 1938 by Swiss chemist Albert Hofmann (1906–). While seeking a headache remedy, Hofmann isolated lysergic acid from the ergot fungus that grows on wheat. In the laboratory he added the diethylamide molecule to the lysergic acid compound. While Hofmann was working with the new compound, a drop of the material entered his bloodstream through the skin of his fingertip and Hofmann soon experienced intense hallucinations.

In the 1950s, American chemists conducted a series of experiments in which the drug was given to mice, spiders, cats, dogs, goats, and an elephant. All of the animals showed dramatic changes in behavior. Experiments on human subjects were then conducted. Researchers hoped to find a use for LSD as a treatment for disorders such as schizophrenia, alcoholism, and narcotic addiction. However, it soon became evident that the drug had no therapeutic (healing) use, and research on it was abandoned.

LSD, an illegal drug, is one of the most potent hallucinogens known. It is 5,000 times more potent than mescaline and 200 times more potent than psilocybin. Just a tiny amount of the drug can produce a dramatic effect. The drug can be swallowed, smoked (mixed with marijuana), injected through a needle, or rubbed on the skin. Taken by mouth, the drug will take about 30 minutes to have any effect and up to an hour for its full effect to be felt. The total effect of LSD can last 6 to 14 hours.

An LSD user will experience blurred vision, dilation of the pupils, and muscle weakness and twitching. Heart rate, blood pressure, and body temperature all increase. The user's perception of colors, distance, shapes, and sizes is totally distorted and constantly changing. Some LSD users claim to be able to taste colors or smell sounds, a mixing of the senses called synesthesia. Hallucinations are common. Mood swings are frequent, with the user alternating between total euphoria and complete despair.

Users have been known to jump off buildings or walk in front of moving trucks because they have lost their grasp of reality. Repeated users of LSD who then stop taking the drug often experience flashbacks, or vivid past hallucinations. How LSD produces all these effects in the body remains unknown. Researchers know that the drug attaches to certain chemical binding sites widely spread throughout the brain. What occurs thereafter is not known.

[*See also* **Addiction**]

Halogens

The halogens are the five chemical elements that make up Group 17 on the periodic table: fluorine, chlorine, bromine, iodine, and astatine. The term halogen comes from Greek terms meaning "to produce sea salt." The halogens are all chemically active. For that reason, none occur naturally in the form of elements. However—with the exception of astatine—they are very widespread and abundant in chemical compounds. The most widely known of these compounds is sodium chloride, or common table salt.

Fluorine and chlorine are gases. Bromine is one of only two liquid elements. Iodine is a solid. Astatine is radioactive and is one of the rarest of the chemical elements. Fluorine is the most reactive of all known elements. Chemical reactivity decreases throughout this family of elements, with fluorine being the most reactive of all known elements, and chlorine, bromine, and iodine being relatively less reactive, respectively.

Simple compounds of the halogens are called halides. When a halogen becomes part of a compound with one other element, its name is changed to an -ide ending; for example, a chloride.

Words to Know

Chemical activity: The tendency to form chemical compounds.

Compound: The combination of two or more elements in a definite mass ratio.

Radioactive: The tendency of an element to break down spontaneously into one or more other elements.

Synthesized: Prepared by scientists in a laboratory; not a naturally occurring process.

Fluorine

The name fluorine comes from the name of the mineral in which the element was found, fluorspar. Fluorine was one of the last common elements to be isolated. It is so reactive that chemists searched for more than 70 years to find a way to extract the element from its compounds. Then, in 1886, French chemist Henri Moissan (1852–1907) found a way to produce fluorine by passing an electric current through a liquid mixture of potassium fluoride and hydrogen fluoride. Moissan's method is still used today, with some modifications, for the production of fluorine.

Properties and uses.   Fluorine is one of the most dangerous chemicals known. It attacks the skin and throat, causing serious burns and respiratory problems at very low concentrations. It is also very reactive chemically. It attacks most chemicals vigorously at room temperature and reacts explosively with water.

An indication of fluorine's reactivity is that it even forms compounds with the family of elements known as the inert gases. The inert gases include helium, neon, argon, krypton, and xenon. They get their name from the fact that they generally do not combine with any other element. However, compounds of xenon and fluorine and krypton and fluorine have been produced. They are the only known compounds of the inert gases to have been discovered.

Because it is so reactive, fluorine itself has few uses. One exception is its role as an oxidizing (burning) agent in rocket fuels. The vast majority of fluorine, however, is used to make compounds. One of the most interesting of those compounds is hydrofluoric acid. This compound has been used since the 1600s to etch glass.

Perhaps the most familiar application of fluorine compounds is in toothpaste additives. Scientists have discovered that the addition of tiny amounts of fluoride in a person's diet can decrease the number of dental caries (cavities) that develop. Today, many kinds of toothpastes include stannous fluoride to improve a person's dental health.

For many years, the most important group of fluorine compounds used commercially were the chlorofluorocarbons (CFCs). The CFCs were developed and used as refrigerants, blowing agents for polyurethane foam, and propellants in spray cans. At one time, more than 700 million kilograms (1.5 billion pounds) of CFCs were produced in a single year.

In the 1980s, however, scientists found that CFCs break down in the atmosphere. The chlorine formed as a result of this breakdown attacks the ozone layer in Earth's stratosphere (the part of Earth's atmosphere that extends 7 to 31 miles [11 to 50 kilometers] above the surface). The loss of the ozone layer is a serious problem for humans since ozone screens out radiation that causes skin cancer and other damage to plants and animals on Earth. Today, scientists are exploring the use of another class of fluorine compounds—the hydrochlorofluorocarbons, or HCFCs—as replacements for CFCs.

Chlorine

Chlorine was first prepared in the 1770s by Swedish chemist Carl Wilhelm Scheele (1742–1786), who thought it was a compound. It was later identified as an element by English chemist Humphry Davy (1778–1829). Davy suggested the name of chlorine for the element because of its greenish-yellow color. (The Greek word for "greenish-yellow" is *chloros.*)

Chlorine occurs most abundantly in sodium chloride, which is obtained from seawater and from underground deposits of rock salt formed from seas that have dried up. To obtain chlorine, an electrical current is passed through brine, a water solution of sodium chloride.

Properties and uses.   Chlorine gas is toxic. It attacks the respiratory tract, causing coughing, congestion, and flu-like symptoms. In high doses, it can be fatal. For this reason, chlorine was used as a chemical weapon during World War I (1914–18).

Chlorine is also very reactive, although less so than fluorine. It forms compounds with almost every other element. Among the most important

Chlorination

The mention of chlorine brings summertime and swimming pools to mind for most people. Chlorine is added to pools and spas to kill bacteria in water that might otherwise cause disease. The process of adding chlorine to a swimming pool is called chlorination. Chlorination is used for other purification purposes also, as in the purification of public water supplies.

Chlorination can be done in various ways. In some cases, gaseous chlorine is pumped directly into water. In other cases, a compound containing chlorine, such as sodium or calcium hypochlorite, is added to water. When that compound breaks down, chlorine and other purifying substances are released to the water.

The term chlorination applies more generally to any chemical reaction in which chlorine is added to some other substance. For example, chlorine and methane gas can be reacted with each other to form a series of chlorine-containing compounds. The best known of that series are trichloromethane (also known as chloroform; used as an anesthetic) and tetrachloromethane (also known as carbon tetrachloride; used as a solvent and a refrigerant).

of those compounds are sodium chloride (table salt), potassium chloride, hydrochloric acid, and calcium chloride.

Chlorine consistently ranks among the top ten chemicals produced in the United States. Some of chlorine's uses depend on its toxic effects. For example, chlorine is now widely used as a disinfectant in municipal water systems, swimming pools, and sewage treatment plants. Many organic (carbon-containing) compounds of chlorine are used as pesticides, herbicides, and fungicides. These compounds kill unwanted insects, weeds, fungi, and other plants and animals. The use of these compounds is often associated with undesirable environmental effects, however. DDT, for example, is a chlorine-containing compound that was once one of the most popular pesticides ever produced. But its harmful effects on fish, birds, and other animals in the environment eventually led to bans on its use in many industrialized nations.

Chlorine is also used in the bleaching of paper, pulp, and textiles. The largest single application of the element is in the preparation of a large variety of compounds, including organic chlorides that are the starting point in the manufacture of plastics and other kinds of polymers (chemical compounds that consist of repeating structural units). One of the most important of these polymers is polyvinyl chloride (PVC), from which plastic pipe and many other plastic products are made. Another is neoprene, a synthetic form of rubber that is resistant to the effects of heat, oxidation, and oils. Neoprene is widely used in automobile parts.

Bromine

Bromine was discovered in 1826 by French chemist Antoine-Jérôme Balard (1802–1876). Balard chose the name bromine from the Greek word for "stink," because of its strong and disagreeable odor. Like chlorine, bromine is obtained from brine. Chlorine gas is used to convert bromide compounds in brine to elemental bromine.

Properties and uses.   Bromine is a beautiful reddish-brown liquid that vaporizes (changes to a gas) easily. The vapors are irritating to the eyes and throat. The liquid is highly corrosive and can cause serious burns if spilled on the skin. Bromine is chemically less active than fluorine and chlorine but more active than iodine.

Like chlorine, bromine can be used as a disinfectant. In fact, some water treatment systems have converted from chlorination to bromination as a way of purifying water. For many years, one of the most important compounds of bromine was ethylene dibromide, an additive in leaded gasolines. Since leaded gasoline has been removed from the market, this use has declined.

The product in which most people are likely to encounter compounds of bromine is in photographic film. Tiny crystals of silver bromide undergo a chemical change when exposed to light. This change is responsible for the image produced when photographic film is used to take a picture.

Bromine is also used to make a number of organic products that function as pesticides. The most popular of these currently is methyl bromide, a fumigant (another word for a substance used to destroy pests). Methyl bromide is used as a spray for potatoes, tomatoes, and other agricultural crops.

The halons are a group of organic compounds that contain bromine along with at least one other halogen. The halons are popular as flame retardants. However, scientists have found that, like the CFCs, they appear to cause damage to Earth's ozone layer. For that reason, their use has been largely reduced throughout the world.

Iodine

Iodine was discovered accidentally in 1811 by French chemist Bernard Courtois (1777–1838). Courtois was burning seaweed to collect potassium nitrate when he noticed that a beautiful violet vapor was produced. When the vapor cooled, it changed to dark, shiny, metallic-like crystals. Humphry Davy later suggested the name iodine for the element from the Greek word *iodos,* for "violet."

As with chlorine and bromine, iodine is obtained from seawater. It can also be produced from Chile saltpeter (sodium nitrate), in which it occurs as an impurity in the form of sodium iodate ($NaIO_3$).

Properties and uses. Iodine vapor is irritating to the eyes and respiratory system. It is highly toxic if ingested. Iodine is the least active of the common halogens (not counting astatine).

The human body uses iodine to make thyroxine, an important hormone (chemical messenger) produced by the thyroid gland. (The thyroid is a gland located in the neck that plays an important role in metabolism—a term used to describe processes of energy production and use by the body.) If insufficient amounts of iodine are present in the diet, a person may develop a condition known as goiter, a sometimes noticeable enlargement of the thyroid gland. Once the relationship between iodine and goiter were first discovered, manufacturers of table salt began to add iodine (in the form of sodium iodide) to their product (iodized salt). This practice has largely eliminated the problem of goiter in modern developed nations.

Iodine is also used commercially in a variety of products including dyes, specialized soaps, lubricants, photographic film, medicines, and pharmaceuticals.

Astatine

Astatine is generally regarded as one of the rarest naturally occurring elements. According to some estimates, no more than 44 milligrams of the element are to be found in Earth's crust. It is hardly surprising, then, that the element was first produced synthetically. In 1940, three physicists at the University of California at Berkeley—D. R. Corson, K. R. Mackenzie, and Emilio Segrè (1905–1989)—made astatine by bombarding the element bismuth with alpha particles in a cyclotron (a particle accelerator or atom-smasher).

About 24 isotopes (forms) of astatine exist, all of them radioactive. The most long-lived has a half-life of 8.3 hours, meaning that half of a sample of the element disappears in 8.3 hours. Because it is so rare and has such a short half-life, astatine is one of the most poorly understood of all chemical elements. It has no practical applications at this time.

[*See also* **Element, chemical; Organic chemistry; Periodic table**]

Hand tools

The earliest hand tools date back to the Old Stone Age (of the Paleolithic period), the earliest period of human development, which started roughly two million years ago. These early hand tools included sticks and rocks picked up and used to pound, dig, or throw. Modern technologies make hand tools that are battery powered, so they are still portable yet easier to use than their predecessors.

Earliest stone and metal tools

Technology begins in human history when the first stone flints or spear tips were deliberately cut. These are known as Oldowan tools or eoliths. It is often difficult for archaeologists to prove that the sharpened edges of some stone artifacts are human-made rather than the result of naturally occurring processes. However, certain improvised tools such as pebbles and animal bones show clear signs of the wear and tear of use. Other tools that have been found with human remains in areas that archaeologists have defined as settlements are clearly human-made.

A plane's basic design has not changed over time. (*Reproduced by permission of Field Mark Publications.*)

About one-and-a-half-million years ago, an improvement was made upon the basic carved tool. The newer tools fall into three categories: hand axes, picks, and cleavers. Hand axes from this period are flaked on both sides and often shaped carefully into teardrops. Picks are long tools, with either one sharp edge or two. Cleavers are smoothed into U-shapes with a sharp point on one side. Archaeologists have a long list of possible uses for these artifacts, which may have served more than one purpose. Butchering animals, digging for roots or water sources, and making other tools are the most common suggestions.

The Bronze Age, which began about 3500 B.C., is the period in human history when metals were first used regularly in the creation of tools and weapons. Metal alloys like bronze were deliberately crafted to improve the durability and efficiency of hand tools. Handcrafted knives were important for nomadic (wandering) peoples who hunted to survive. Swords became crucial tools in warfare. The invention of the metal plow brought agriculture a huge step forward, since it made systematic planting over wide areas possible.

Development of modern tools

Some hand tools have gone out of style or are used only rarely. The cobbler (old term for shoemaker) used to make shoes by hand, but now people buy mass-produced shoes and only take them to a repair shop to be worked on by hand. However, a sewing needle has not changed in centuries—it is still a common household object. Even though people now have access to big sewing machines, it is still easier to fix a button or darn a small tear with a plain needle.

During colonial times only the metal parts of a tool would be sold to a user, who would then make his own handle out of wood to fit in his hand perfectly. Many things made with metal nowadays, like nails and shovels, were then made from wood. This is why older buildings and tools have aged well, without problems such as rusting.

Modern technology

Simple hand tools, which cut, pound, or assemble, are now sold with attached metal or plastic handles. Their basic designs and operations, however, have not changed over time. Drills are still used to bore holes, saws to cut hard materials, screwdrivers to attach screws, wrenches to tighten nuts and bolts, and planes and files to smooth down metal or wood surfaces. Some of these tools, such as drills and saws, are now primarily electric, which saves time and effort. Other present-day tools combine modern technology with time-tested operation. Squares and levels now measure inclines and angles with liquid crystal digital displays, but they otherwise look, feel, and perform like their old-fashioned counterparts.

Heart

In humans, the heart is a pulsating organ that pumps blood throughout the body. On average, the heart weighs about 10.5 ounces (300 grams). It is a four-chambered, cone-shaped organ about the size of a closed fist. It lies under the sternum (breastbone), nestled between the lungs. The

Words to Know

Angina pectoris: Chest pain that occurs when blood flow to the heart is reduced, resulting in a shortage of oxygen.

Aorta: Largest blood vessel in the body.

Atherosclerosis: Condition in which fatty material such as cholesterol accumulates on an artery wall forming plaque that obstructs blood flow.

Atrioventricular node: Area of specialized tissue that lies near the bottom of the right atrium that fires an electrical impulse across the ventricles, causing them to contract.

Atria: Upper heart chambers that receive blood.

Diastole: Period of relaxation and expansion of the heart when its chambers fill with blood.

Mitral valve: Valve with two cusps that separates the left atrium from the left ventricle.

Pericardium: Fibrous sac that encloses the heart.

Sinoatrial node: Area of specialized tissue in the upper area of the right atrium that fires an electrical impulse across the atria, causing them to contract.

Systole: Rhythmic contraction of the heat.

Tricuspid valve: Fibrous, three-leaflet valve that separates the right atrium from the right ventricle.

Ventricles: Lower heart chambers that pump blood.

heart is covered by a triple-layered, fibrous sac called the pericardium. This important organ is protected within a bony cage formed by the ribs, sternum, and spine.

In its ceaseless work, the heart contracts more than 100,000 times a day to drive blood through about 60,000 miles (96,000 kilometers) of vessels to nourish each of the trillions of cells in the body. Each contraction of the heart forces about 2.5 ounces (74 milliliters) of blood into the bloodstream. This adds up to about 10 pints (4.7 liters) of blood every minute. An average heart will pump about 1,800 gallons (6,800 liters) of blood each day. With exercise, that amount may increase as much as six times.

In an average lifetime, the heart will pump about 100 million gallons (380 million liters) of blood.

The heart is divided into four chambers. The upper chambers are the atria (singular atrium). The lower chambers are the ventricles. The wall that divides the right and left sides of the heart is the septum. The atria are thin-walled holding chambers for blood that returns to the heart from the body. The ventricles are muscular chambers that contract rhythmically to propel blood through the body.

Movement of blood between chambers and in and out of the heart is controlled by valves that allow movement in only one direction. Between the atria and ventricles are atrioventricular (AV) valves. Between the ventricles and the major arteries into which they pump blood are semilunar (SL) valves. The "lub-dup" sounds that a physician hears through a stethoscope occur when the heart valves close. The AV valves produce the "lub" sound upon closing, while the SL valves cause the "dup" sound.

Movement of blood through the heart

Blood carrying no oxygen (oxygen-depleted) returns to the right atrium of the heart through the vena cava, a major vein. It then passes through the tricuspid or right AV valve into the right ventricle. The tricuspid valve is so named because it has three cusps or flaps that open and close to control the flow of blood. When the right ventricle contracts, blood is forced from the heart into the pulmonary artery through the pulmonary SL valve.

The pulmonary artery is the only artery in the body that carries oxygen-depleted blood. It carries this blood into the lungs, where the blood releases carbon dioxide and other impurities and picks up oxygen. The freshly oxygenated blood then returns to the left atrium through the four pulmonary veins. The blood then passes through the mitral or left AV valve into the left ventricle.

The left ventricle has the hardest task of any chamber in the heart. It must force blood from the heart into the body and head. For that purpose it has a much thicker wall, approximately three times thicker than the wall of the right ventricle. When the left ventricle contracts, blood passes through the aortic SL valve into the largest artery in the body— the aorta—to be carried and distributed to every area of the body.

The heart muscle or myocardium is unique in that it is not under voluntary control (a person cannot cause it to start and stop at will) and it must work without ceasing for a lifetime. The myocardium requires a great deal of nourishment, and the arteries that feed it are the first to branch off from the aorta. These coronary arteries pass down and over the heart, providing it with an abundant and uninterrupted blood supply.

The heart cycle and nerve impulses

Each heartbeat or heart cycle (also known as the cardiac cycle) is divided into two phases. The two atria contract while the two ventricles relax. Then, the two ventricles contract while the two atria relax. The contraction phase is known as systole, while the relaxation phase is known as diastole. The heart cycle consists of a systole and diastole of both the atria and ventricles. At the end of a heartbeat all four chambers rest.

The pattern of heart chambers filling and emptying in sequence is controlled by a system of nerve fibers. They provide the electrical stimulus to trigger contraction of the heart muscle. The initial stimulant is provided by a small strip of specialized tissue in the upper area of the right atrium. This is called the sinoatrial or SA node. The SA node fires an electrical impulse that spreads across the atria, causing them to contract. The impulse also reaches another node, the atrioventricular or AV node. (The AV node lies near the bottom of the right atrium just above the ventricle.) After receiving the SA impulse, the AV node sends out its own electrical impulse. The AV impulse travels down a specialized train of fibers into the ventricular muscle, causing the ventricles to contract. In this way, the contraction of the atria occur slightly before the contraction of the ventricles.

The electrical activity of the heart can be measured by a device called the electrocardiograph (EKG). Variations in the heart's electrical system can lead to serious, even dangerous, consequences. When that occurs, an electrical stimulator called an artificial pacemaker must be implanted to take over the regulation of the heartbeat. The small pacemaker can be implanted under the skin near the shoulder. Long wires from the pacemaker are fed into the heart and implanted in the heart muscle. The pacemaker can be regulated for the number of heartbeats it will stimulate per minute. Newer pacemakers can detect the need for increased heart rate when the individual is exercising or under stress.

Heart diseases

Heart disease is the number-one cause of death among people living in the industrial world. Preventive measures, such as an improved diet and regular exercise, are the best methods to overcome heart disease.

Congenital heart disease is any defect in the heart present at birth. About 1 out of every 100 infants are born with some sort of heart abnormality. Many of these congenital defects do not need to be treated.

The most common type of congenital heart disease is the atrial septal defect. In this condition, an opening in the septum between the right and left atria allows blood from the two chambers to mix. If the hole is small, it does not cause a problem. But a larger opening that allows too much blood to mix can cause the right ventricle to be overwhelmed with blood,

A cutaway view of the anatomy of the heart (top) and a diagram showing blood flow in the heart during diastole (relaxation) and systole (contraction). *(Reproduced by permission of The Gale Group.)*

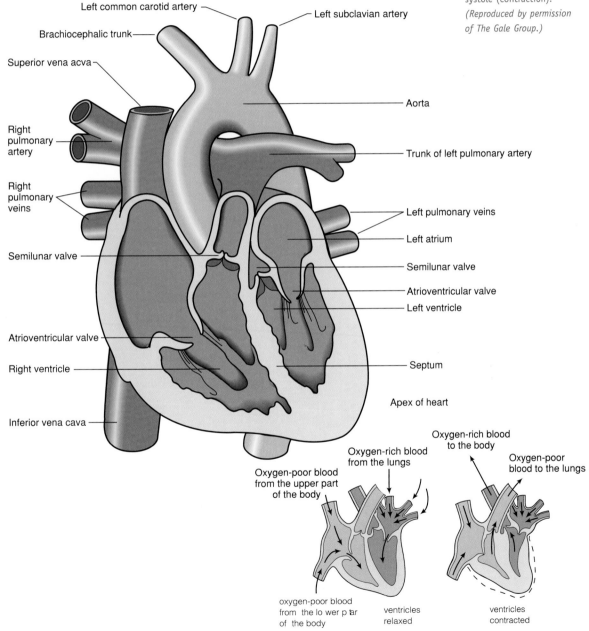

Left common carotid artery

Left subclavian artery

Brachiocephalic trunk

Superior vena acva

Aorta

Right pulmonary artery

Trunk of left pulmonary artery

Right pulmonary veins

Left pulmonary veins

Left atrium

Semilunar valve

Semilunar valve

Atrioventricular valve

Left ventricle

Atrioventricular valve

Right ventricle

Septum

Apex of heart

Inferior vena cava

Oxygen-rich blood to the body

Oxygen-rich blood from the lungs

Oxygen-poor blood to the lungs

Oxygen-poor blood from the upper part of the body

oxygen-poor blood from the lower part of the body

ventricles relaxed

ventricles contracted

a condition that eventually leads to heart failure. The defect can be corrected through a surgical procedure in which a patch is placed over the opening to seal it.

Coronary heart disease (also known as coronary artery disease) is the most common form of heart disease. A condition known as atherosclerosis results when fatty material such as cholesterol accumulates on an artery wall forming plaque that obstructs blood flow. When the obstruction occurs in one of the main arteries leading to the heart, the heart

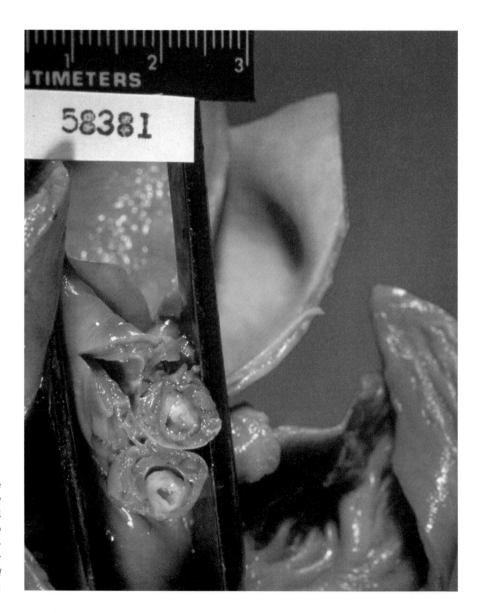

The build-up of white plaque in the coronary arteries of this individual allows very little blood to flow through them. The condition can lead to angina or a heart attack. *(Reproduced by permission of Phototake.)*

does not receive enough blood and oxygen and its muscle cells begin to die. The primary symptom of this condition is pain in the upper left part of the chest that radiates down the left arm—what is called angina pectoris. A heart attack (myocardial infarction) occurs when blood flow to the heart is completely blocked.

Numerous types of drugs have been developed to treat patients with heart disease. Some drugs are given to make the heart beat more slowly, removing stress placed on it. Other drugs cause blood vessels to dilate or stretch. This also reduces stress on the heart. A third important type of drug reduces cholesterol in the blood.

Surgical procedures are often used to treat heart disease. One procedure is known as coronary bypass surgery. To supply blood to the coronary artery beyond the point of blockage, blood vessels are taken from other parts of the body (often the leg) and connected to the artery. Another commonly performed procedure is angioplasty, during which narrowed arteries are stretched to enable blood to flow more easily. The surgery involves threading a balloon catheter (tube) through the coronary artery and then stretching the artery by inflating the balloon.

The most dramatic treatment for heart disease is the replacement of damaged hearts with healthy human or even animal hearts. The first successful human heart transplant was performed by South African surgeon Christiaan Barnard (1922–)in 1967. The patient, however, died in 18 days. Many patients who received early heart transplants died days or months after the operation, mostly because their bodies rejected the new organ. In the early 1980s, effective drugs were developed to fight organ rejection. By the late-1990s, the one-year survival rate of patients receiving heart transplants was over 81 percent. For those who survived the first year, survival rates rose to over 90 percent.

[*See also* **Circulatory system; Electrocardiogram; Transplant, surgical**]

Heat

Heat is the energy that flows between two objects because of a difference in temperature. Heat always flows from a body at a higher temperature to one at a lower temperature.

Scientists use the term heat differently than do nonscientists. The average person may think of heat as the amount of energy contained in a body. The correct term for that property, however, is thermal energy.

Heat Transfer

Another way to think of heat is as a transfer of thermal energy from one place to another. This process occurs in one of three ways: conduction, convection, and radiation.

Conduction. Conduction is the process of heat transfer. Rapidly moving molecules in a hot material collide with slower moving molecules in a cool material. The fast-moving molecules slow down and the slow-moving molecules increase their speed. Conduction occurs, then, when two bodies of different temperatures are in contact with each other.

Convection. Convection is the process by which large masses of a fluid (a liquid or gas) move, carrying thermal energy. When water in a container is heated, for example, it expands. Cooler water around it pushes the lighter water upward. As the warm water rises, it begins to cool and starts to move downward in the liquid again. Eventually, a circular motion is produced within the liquid, forcing heat to be transferred throughout the liquid.

Radiation. Finally, thermal energy can be transferred by radiation. Hot bodies emit electromagnetic radiation that corresponds to their temperature. This radiation passes through space until it comes into contact with a body with less thermal energy. The cooler body then absorbs this radiation and becomes warmer.

Thermal energy and temperature

According to the kinetic theory of matter, all matter is composed of particles that are constantly in motion. Temperature is a measure of the motion of those particles. The more rapidly particles are in motion, the higher the temperature; the less rapidly they are moving, the lower the temperature.

In theory, it would be possible to reduce the motion of the particles in an object to zero. In that case, the object would contain no thermal energy. The temperature at which all particle motion ends is called absolute zero. Scientists have come within a few millionths of a degree of absolute zero but have never actually reached that point.

Transfer of thermal energy. The transfer of thermal energy from one place to another occurs in one of three ways: conduction, convection, and radiation. In conduction, rapidly moving molecules in a hot material collide with slower moving molecules in a cool material. The fast-moving molecules slow down and the slow-moving molecules increase their speed. Conduction occurs, then, when two bodies of different temperatures are in contact with each other.

Convection is the process by which large masses of a fluid (a liquid or gas) move, carrying thermal energy. When water in a container is heated, for example, it expands. Cooler water around it pushes the lighter water upward. As the warm water rises, it begins to cool and starts to move downward in the liquid again. Eventually, a circular motion is produced within the liquid, forcing heat to be transferred throughout the liquid.

Finally, thermal energy can be transferred by radiation. Hot bodies emit electromagnetic radiation that corresponds to their temperature. This radiation passes through space until it comes into contact with a body with less thermal energy. The cooler body then absorbs this radiation and becomes warmer.

Heat units

Since heat is a form of energy, the units used to measure heat are the same as those used to measure energy. In the metric system, one of the earliest units used to measure heat was the calorie. The calorie is defined as the amount of heat energy needed to raise the temperature of one gram of water one degree Celsius. To be precise, the temperature change is specified as an increase from 14.5°C to 15.5°C.

In the International System of Units (the SI system), the unit of energy is the joule. A calorie is defined as 4.184 joules.

Specific heat

Materials differ from each other with regard to how easily they can be warmed. One could add a joule of heat to a gram of water, a gram of iron, a gram of mercury, and a gram of ethyl alcohol and notice very different results. The temperature of the mercury would rise the most, and the temperature of the water would rise the least.

The specific heat capacity (or just specific heat) of a material is defined as the amount of heat required to raise the temperature of one gram of the material one degree Celsius. It takes 4.18 joules to raise the temperature of 1 gram of water 1 degree Celsius (at a temperature of 25°C). In comparison, it takes only 0.14 joule to raise the temperature of the same amount of mercury by one degree Celsius and 0.45 joule to raise the temperature of the same amount of iron by one degree Celsius. It takes 2.46 joules to raise the temperature of the same amount of ethyl alcohol by one degree Celsius.

[*See also* **Energy; Temperature; Thermodynamics**]

Hibernation

Hibernation is a state of inactivity, in which an animal's heart rate, body temperature, and breathing rate are decreased in order to conserve energy through the cold months of winter. A similar state, known as estivation, occurs in some desert animals during the dry months of summer.

Hibernation is a technique that animals have developed in order to adapt to harsh climates. When food is scarce, an animal may use up more energy maintaining its body temperature and in searching for food than it would receive from consuming the food. Hibernating animals use 70 to 100 times less energy than when active, allowing them to survive until food is once again plentiful.

Many animals sleep more often when food is scarce, but only a few truly hibernate. Hibernation differs from sleep in that a hibernating animal shows a drastic reduction in metabolism, and then awakes relatively slowly. (Metabolism is the process by which cells in an organism break down compounds to produce energy.) By contrast, a sleeping animal decreases its metabolism only slightly, and can wake up almost instantly if disturbed. Also, hibernating animals do not show periods of rapid eye movement (REM), the stage of sleep associated with dreaming in humans.

Bears, which many people think of as the classic hibernating animals, are actually just deep sleepers. They do not significantly lower their metabolism and body temperature. True hibernation occurs only in small mammals, such as bats and woodchucks, and a few birds, such as poorwills and nighthawks. Some species of insects show periods of inactivity during which growth and development cease and metabolism is greatly reduced. This state is generally referred to as diapause, although when correlated with the winter months, it would also fit the definition of hibernation.

Preparing for hibernation

Animals prepare for hibernation in the fall by storing enough food to last them until spring. Chipmunks accomplish this task by filling their burrows with food, which they consume during periodic arousals from hibernation throughout the winter. Most animals, however, store energy internally, as fat. A woodchuck in early summer may have only about 5 percent body fat. However, as fall approaches, changes occur in the animal's brain chemistry that cause it to feel hungry and to eat constantly. As a result, the woodchuck's body fat increases to about 15 percent of its total weight. In other animals, such as the dormouse, fat may comprise as much as 50 percent of the animal's weight by the time hibernation begins. A short period of fasting usually follows the feeding frenzy, to ensure that the digestive tract is completely emptied before hibernation begins.

Entering hibernation

Going into hibernation is a gradual process. Over a period of days, an animal's heart rate and breathing rate drop slowly, eventually

A year in the life of a female arctic ground squirrel. *(Reproduced by permission of The Gale Group.)*

Between July and September, the arctic ground squirrel gains weight in preparation for hibernation and spends time storing food and insulating its burrow with grass and hair.

The young leave the burrow in mid-July, and by October already weigh as much as the adults.

Females bear their young in the middle of June, after a 25-day gestation period.

Mating occurs in mid-May.

It enters hibernation in late September or early October by going through stages of torpor (inactivity) and arousal which gradually lower its body temperature.

Deeply hibernating, the squirrel takes only three irregular breaths per minute. Its body temperature is near or slightly below freezing, and its heart beats only three or four times per minute.

The squirrel may awaken every two or three weeks to move about, eat some stored food, or even venture to the surface.

Awakening takes about three hours. About 40% of the squirrel's total body weight is lost during the period of hibernation.

reaching rates of just a few times per minute. Their body temperature also drops from levels of 37° to 38°C (99° to 100°F) to 10° to 20°C (50° to 70°F). The lowered body temperature makes fewer demands on metabolism and food stores.

Electrical activity in the brain almost completely ceases during hibernation, although some areas remain active. These areas are those that respond to external stimuli such as light, temperature, and noise. Thus, the hibernating animal can be aroused under extreme conditions.

Arousal

Periodically, perhaps every two weeks or so, the hibernating animal awakes and takes a few deep breaths to refresh its air supply, or in the case of the chipmunk, to grab a bite to eat. If the weather is particularly mild, some animals may venture above ground. These animals, including chipmunks, skunks, and raccoons, are sometimes called shallow hibernators.

Arousal begins with an increase in the heart rate. Blood vessels dilate, particularly around the heart, lungs and brain, leading to an increased breathing rate. Eventually, the increase in circulation and metabolic activity spreads throughout the body, reaching the hindquarters last. It usually takes several hours for the animal to become fully active.

[*See also* **Metabolism**]

Hologram and holography

Holography is a method of producing a three-dimensional (3-D) image of an object. (The three dimensions are height, width, and depth.) The image it brings to life is referred to as a hologram, from the Greek word meaning "whole picture." Unlike a two-dimensional picture, a hologram allows a person to look "around" and "behind" its subject.

The hologram is actually a recording of the difference between two beams of coherent light. Light is composed of waves that are all the same length and that travel in all directions. Coherent light is in phase, meaning its waves are vibrating and traveling together in the same direction. To create a hologram, a laser beam (coherent light) is split in two: one beam that stays undisturbed, called the reference beam, strikes a photographic plate. The second beam, called the object beam, strikes the subject and then bounces onto the plate. The subject's interfering with the second beam causes the two beams to become out of phase. This difference—called phase interference—is what is recorded on the photographic plate. When a hologram is later illuminated with coherent light of the same frequency that created it, a three-dimensional image of the subject appears.

Birth of the hologram

In 1947, English physicist Dennis Gabor (1900–1979) tried to improve the image-producing capability of electron microscopes, which use streams of electrons rather than light to magnify objects. His solution was

A hologram of the Venus de Milo. *(Reproduced by permission of Photo Researchers, Inc.)*

to take an electron "picture" of an object. However, this process required a coherent light source—something that did not exist at the time. It wasn't until the early 1960s, when the first working laser was produced, that 3-D images could be created. For developing the basic principles of holography, Gabor was awarded the Nobel Prize in 1971.

Uses for holograms

One of the most visible applications of holography is in the field of advertising. Holograms can be found on the covers of magazines, books, and music recordings. In the 1970s, automakers would often use cylindrical holograms to show a new car model. A prospective car buyer could walk around the tube and view the vehicle from all angles, though the cylinder was actually empty.

The medical field was also quick to find a use for holograms. A holographic picture could be taken for research, enabling many doctors to examine a subject in three dimensions. Also, holograms can "jump" mediums, that is, a hologram made using X rays can be viewed later in white light with increased magnification and depth. Holography has also been instrumental in the development of acoustical (sound) imaging and is often used in place of X-ray spectroscopy, especially during pregnancies.

A critical application of holography is in computer data storage. Magnetic disks, the most common storage device for home and small-frame computers, is two dimensional, so its storage capacity is limited. Because of its three-dimensional nature, a hologram can store much more information. Optical memories store large amounts of binary data (with series of zeroes and ones representing bits of information) on groupings of small holograms. When viewed by the computer using coherent light, these groupings reveal a 3-D image full of information.

Credit companies now use holographic images on their credit cards. Since holograms are expensive and difficult to produce, the practice discourages counterfeiting.

[*See also* **Laser; Spectroscopy**]

Hormones

Hormones are chemicals produced by one kind of tissue in an organism and then transported to other tissues in the organism, where they produce some kind of response. Because of the way they operate, hormones are

Words to Know

Auxins: A group of plant hormones responsible for patterns of plant growth.

Endocrine glands: Glands that produce and release hormones in an animal.

Phototropism: The tendency of a plant to grow towards a source of light.

Plant growth regulators: Plant hormones that affect the rate at which plants grow.

sometimes called "chemical messengers." Hormones are very different from each other—depending on the functions they perform—and they occur in both plants and animals.

An example of hormone action is the chemical known as vasopressin. Vasopressin is produced in the pituitary gland (at the base of the brain) of animals and then excreted into the bloodstream. The hormone travels to the kidneys, where it causes an increase in water retention. Greater water retention produces, in turn, an increase in blood pressure.

Plant hormones

Some of the earliest research on hormones involved plants. In the 1870s, English naturalist Charles Darwin (1809–1882) and his son Francis (1848–1925) studied the effect of light on plant growth. They discovered that plants tend to grow towards a source of light. They called the process phototropism. The reason for this effect was not discovered for another half century. Then, in the 1920s, Dutch-American botanist Frits Went (1863–1935) discovered the presence of certain compounds that control the growth of plant tips toward light. Went named those compounds auxins. Auxins are formed in the green tips of growing plants, in root tips, and on the shaded side of growing shoots. They alter the rate at which various cells in the plant grow so that it always bends towards the light.

Many other plant hormones have since been discovered. These hormones are also called plant growth regulators because they affect the rate at which roots, stems, leaves, or other plant parts grow. The gibberellins,

Important Hormones of the Human Body

Hormone	Source	Function
Adrenalin (epinephrine)	Adrenal gland	Initiates emergency "fight or flight" responses in the nervous system
Androgens (including testosterone)	Testes	Develop and maintain sex organs and male secondary sex characteristics
Cortisone and related hormones	Adrenal gland	Control the metabolism (breaking down) of carbohydrates and proteins (to produce energy), maintain proper balance of electrolytes (which regulate the electric charge and flow of water molecules across cell membranes), and reduce inflammation
Digestive hormones	Various parts of the digestive system	Make possible various stages of digestion
Estrogen	Ovaries and uterus	Develops sex organs and secondary female sexual characteristics; maintains pregnancy
Glucagon	Pancreas (Islets of Langerhans)	Raises blood glucose (sugar) levels
Gonadotropic hormones	Pituitary gland	Stimulate gonads (sex organs)
Growth hormone	Pituitary gland	Stimulates growth of skeleton and gain in body weight
Insulin	Pancreas (Islets of Langerhans)	Lowers blood glucose levels
Oxytocin	Pituitary gland	Causes contraction of some smooth muscles
Progesterone	Ovaries and uterus	Influences menstrual cycle and maintains pregnancy
Thyroxine	Thyroid gland	Regulates rate of metabolism and general growth rate
Vasopressin	Pituitary gland	Reduces loss of water from kidneys

for example, are chemicals that occur in many different kinds of plants. They cause cells to divide (reproduce) more quickly and to grow larger in size. Another group of plant growth regulators is the cytokinins. One interesting effect of the cytokinins is that they tend to prevent leaves from aging. When placed on a yellow leaf, a drop of cytokinin can cause the leaf to turn green again.

Animal hormones

Hundreds of different hormones have been discovered in animals. The human body alone contains more than 100 different hormones. These hormones are secreted by endocrine glands, also known as ductless glands. Examples of endocrine glands include the hypothalamus, pituitary gland, pineal gland, thyroid, parathyroid, thymus, adrenals, pancreas, ovaries, and testes. Hormones are secreted from these glands directly into the bloodstream. They then travel to target tissues and regulate digestion, growth, maturation, reproduction, and homeostasis (maintaining the body's chemical balance).

[*See also* **Diabetes mellitus; Endocrine system; Reproductive system; Stress**]

A garden of perennials.
(*Reproduced by permission of Photo Researchers, Inc.*)

Horticulture

Horticulture is the science and art of growing and caring for plants, especially flowers, fruits, and vegetables. Whereas agronomy (a branch of agriculture) refers to the growing of field crops, horticulture refers to small-scale gardening. The word horticulture comes from Latin and means "garden cultivation."

Within the field of horticulture, seed growers, plant growers, and nurseries are the major suppliers of plant products. Among the important specialists who work in the field of horticulture are plant physiologists, who work on the nutritional needs of plants, and plant entomologists, who work to protect plants from insect damage.

Horticulturists are often involved in the landscaping and maintenance of public gardens, parks, golf courses, and ball fields. For the amateur home gardener, the rewards are both recreational and emotional. Gardening is one of the most popular pastimes for people—not only for those living in suburbs, but for city dwellers who plant window boxes, grow house plants, or develop a garden in an empty city lot.

Human evolution

Since the mid-nineteenth century, Western scientific thought has stated that all present-day species on Earth, including man, have arisen from earlier, simpler forms of life. This theory means that the story of human evolution begins with a creature most people today would not consider human.

In 1859, the view of man's history and his place on Earth was changed forever by the publication of *On the Origin of Species by Means of Natural Selection,* written by English naturalist Charles Darwin (1809–1882). In this revolutionary book, Darwin stated that all living things achieved their present form through a long period of natural changes. In his 1871 book, *The Descent of Man,* Darwin further argued that man descended from subhuman forms of life.

The history of how the human species evolved has been reconstructed by evidence gathered by paleontologists (who study fossils), anthropologists (who study humans and their origins, development, and customs), anatomists (who study the structure of biological organisms), biochemists (who study chemical compounds and processes occurring in biological organisms), and many other scientists. Most of the concrete evidence comes from the record left by fossils, which are remains or imprints of ancient plants or animals that are found in layers of rock. In practice, human fossils are mostly bones and teeth, which are the parts of the human body more likely to be preserved over a great time period.

The human fossil record

In the overall history of life on Earth, the human species is a very recent product of evolution. There are no humanlike fossils older than 4.4 million years, which makes them only one-thousandth the age of life on Earth.

The human species, or *Homo sapiens,* belongs to the hominid family tree. Hominid means "human types," and describes early creatures who split off from the apes and took to walking upright or on their hind legs. Studies have shown that *Homo sapiens* share a clear anatomical and ge-

▼ **Words to Know**

Fossils: Remains or imprints of ancient plants or animals that are found in layers of rock.

Hominid: Member of the family of primates that includes modern humans.

Primate: Member of the group of mammals that includes lemurs, monkeys, apes, and humans.

netic relationship to other primates (members of the group of mammals that includes lemurs, monkeys, apes, and humans). Of all the primates, humans have the closest relationship with apes. Both species have descended from a common ancestor. At some point in evolution, the branch of primates split into two arms. One evolved into modern apes, while the other evolved into modern humans.

The reasons that human ancestors started to walk upright are not known. Possibly, it was a response to environmental changes; as tropical forests were beginning to shrink, walking might have been a better way to cross the grasslands to get to nearby patches of forest for food. Standing upright also may have been a means of defense that slowly evolved. When chimpanzees or gorillas become excited, they stand in an upright posture and shake a stick or throw an object. By standing upright, they appear bigger and more impressive in size than they normally are. In addition, the ability to stand up and get a wider view of the surroundings gives an animal an advantage in the tall grasses. Walking upright also frees up the hands to carry objects, such as tools.

Australopithecus. One of the oldest known humanlike animals to have walked upright is believed to be *Australopithecus afarensis,* meaning the southern ape of the Afar region in Ethiopia, Africa, where the fossils were found. The most famous of these fossils, nicknamed Lucy, was found in 1974 near Hadar, Ethiopia, by a team of anthropologists led by American Donald Johanson (1943–). Lucy lived about 3.18 million years ago, and had a skull, knees, and a pelvis more similar to humans than to apes. Her brain size was about one-third that of modern humans, yet larger than any apelike ancestor to have come before. She would have stood about 3.5 feet (1 meter) tall, with long arms, a V-shaped jaw, and a large projecting face.

In 1924, Australian anthropologist Raymond Dart (1893–1988) discovered fossils at a site called Taung in South Africa. These fossils, dated at 3 million years old, were named *Australopithecus africanus,* meaning the southern ape of Africa. *Australopithecus africanus* probably evolved from *Australopithecus afarensis,* but was slightly taller and had a slightly larger brain. Altogether, there were probably four main species of australopithecines.

Kenyanthropus. In early 2001, discoverers and scientists of human evolution were stunned by the announcement of the discovery of a 3.5 million-year-old skull from what appeared to be an entirely new branch of the early human family tree. The skull was discovered in 1999 by a research team led by Meave Leakey on the western side of Lake Turkana in northern Kenya. Leakey named the new member of the hominid family *Kenyanthropus platyops,* meaning flat-faced man of Kenya. With a flattened face and small molars, this hominid differed significantly from the contemporary species to which Lucy belonged. This discovery has led paleontologists to theorize that the human family tree is not one with a straight trunk, but one shaped more like a complex bush with a tangle of branches leading in many directions. Some branches lead to other branches, while some lead to dead ends.

Homo. From one of these previous branches came the oldest known hominid given the Latin name *Homo,* or "man." This was *Homo habilis,* or "handy man." Discovered by English archaeologist and anthropologist Louis S. B. Leakey (1903–1972) in 1961 in Olduvai Gorge, Tanzania, this hominid was present in east Africa at least 2 million years ago. Taller than his predecessors, *Homo habilis* showed the first marked expansion of the brain. He was the first hominid to use tools routinely.

By about 1.6 million years ago, the hominid brain had increased to about one-half the size of what it is today, and this difference made for a new classification, *Homo erectus,* or "upright man." *Homo erectus* is generally thought to have been modern man's direct ancestor. The first known fossil of *Homo erectus* was found by Dutch paleontologist Eugène Dubois (1858–1940) in 1894 in Java (an island of Indonesia); it was nicknamed Java man. *Homo erectus* is believed to have lived between 250,000 and 1.6 million years ago, although recent scientific findings on Java indicate that *Homo erectus* may have lived there until about 27,000 to 53,000 years ago. *Homo erectus* was the first hominid to use fire and hand axes.

Anthropologists have long agreed that the first humans arose in Africa. Just when these early humans began to migrate out of Africa and inhabit other continents, however, has been a matter of fierce debate. But

Opposite Page: The fossil skeleton of Lucy, the *Australopithecus afarensis* specimen Donald Johanson's team unearthed in 1974 near Hadar, Ethiopia. Lucy lived about 3.18 million years ago, and had a skull, knees, and a pelvis more similar to humans than to apes. *(Reproduced by permission of Photo Researchers, Inc.)*

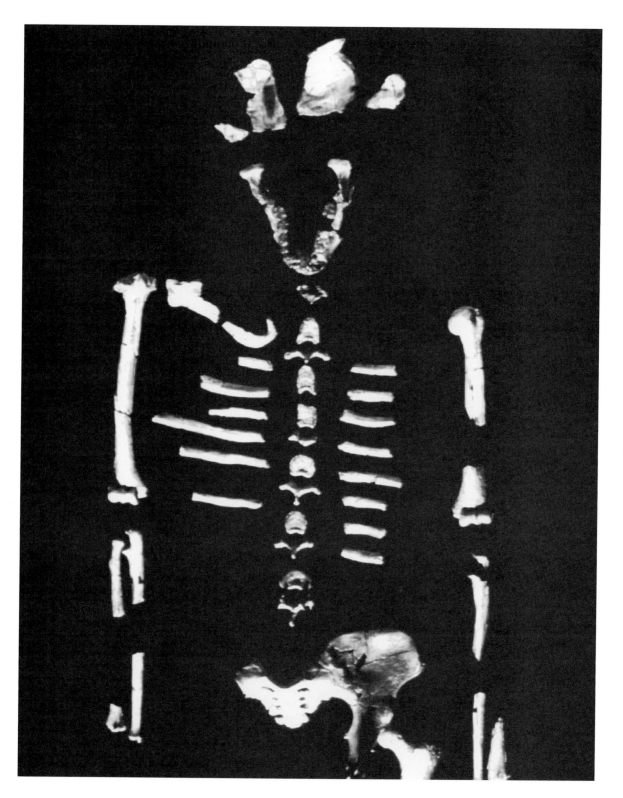

in May 2000, a team of anthropologists reported the first undisputed proof that humans indeed left Africa at least 1.7 million years ago. The team found two well-preserved skulls about 53 miles (85 kilometers) south of Tbilisi, the capital of the Asian nation of Georgia. The skulls closely resembled those of an early human species—called *Homo ergaster* by some scientists and early *Homo erectus* by others—known to have lived in Africa between 1.9 million and 1.4 million years ago. Scientists say the find demonstrates that *Homo ergaster* was on the move shortly after this new species arose in Africa and that some of our earliest ancestors were already restless wanderers.

Homo sapiens. Between 250,000 and 400,000 years ago, *Homo erectus* evolved into *Homo sapiens* ("wise man"). These ancestors of modern man cooked their food, wore clothing, buried their dead, and constructed shelters, but did not have a modern-sized brain. Over time, the body and brain of *Homo sapiens* gradually became somewhat larger.

By about 40,000 years ago, *Homo sapiens* had evolved into modern human beings, *Homo sapiens sapiens* ("wise, wise man"). In 1868, the first fossils of modern *Homo sapiens sapiens* were found in Cro-Magnon caves in southwest France, which gave that name to all early *Homo sapiens sapiens.* Cro-Magnon remains have been found along with the skeletons of woolly mammoth, bison, and reindeer and with tools made from bone, antler, ivory, stone, and wood, indicating that Cro-Magnon hunted game of all sizes. Cro-Magnon buried their dead with body ornaments such as necklaces, beaded clothing, and bracelets.

Cro-Magnon were artists, producing hauntingly beautiful cave art. Carefully rendered pictures of animals, human and mythical representations, and geometric shapes and symbols were created using charcoal and other pigments. Carvings of stone, ivory, and bone have also been discovered in these caves.

In the late twentieth century, new fossil discoveries and genetic evidence fueled a debate concerning when and where *Homo sapiens sapiens* emerged. In 1988, researchers found fossil fragments in a cave in Israel that suggest that anatomically modern humans lived there 92,000 years ago. These findings support the theory that modern humans existed much longer than previously believed. They also support the theory, called the out-of-Africa model, that modern humans evolved only once, in Africa, leaving there in a rapid global expansion to replace other populations of older human forms in Europe and Asia. The out-of-Africa model is opposed by the multiregional model, which argues that modern humans arose almost simultaneously and independently in several different places in Africa, Europe, and Asia.

Neanderthal man

Neanderthal man (*Homo sapiens neanderthalensis*) was the first human fossil to be found in modern times. It was discovered in 1856 in Germany's Neander Valley. These early humanlike hominids (the source of the caveman stereotype) had a large brain, a strong upper body, a bulbous nose, and a prominent brow ridge. They were proficient hunters. It is possible that Neanderthals had an elaborate culture, were aware of the medicinal properties of plants, and ritually buried their dead. Neanderthals first appeared 300,000 years ago in what is now Europe, lived throughout the ice ages, and disappeared about 35,000 years ago.

Recent excavations in Israel show that Neanderthals were contemporary with modern *Homo sapiens sapiens*. The two hominids apparently

The different stages of evolution, from ape to *Homo sapiens sapiens*. (*Reproduced by permission of Custom Medical Stock Photo, Inc.*)

survived independently of each other for thousands of years. In 1997, a team of German biologists analyzed the DNA (deoxyribonucleic acid; genetic material) extracted from the bones of a Neanderthal who lived at least 30,000 years ago. Their findings indicated that Neanderthals did not interbreed with modern humans. The findings also suggested that the Neanderthal line is four times older than the modern human line, meaning Neanderthals split off much earlier from the hominid line than did the ancestors of modern humans. Scientists do not know why Neanderthals died out, nor what the nature of their interaction with *Homo sapiens sapiens* might have been.

[*See also* **Evolution; Fossil and fossilization; Genetics; Primates**]

Human Genome Project

The Human Genome Project is the scientific research effort to construct a complete map of all of the genes carried in human chromosomes. The finished blueprint of human genetic information will serve as a basic reference for research in human biology and will provide insights into the genetic basis of human disease.

Fifteen-year federal project

The human "genome" is the word used to describe the complete collection of genes found in a single set of human chromosomes. It was in the early 1980s that medical and technical advances first suggested to biologists that a project was possible that would locate, identify, and find out what each of the 100,000 or so genes that make up the human body actually do. After investigations by two United States government agencies—the Department of Energy and the National Institutes of Health—the U.S. Congress voted to support a fifteen-year project, and on October 1, 1990, the Human Genome Project officially began. It was to be coordinated with the existing related programs in several other countries. The project's official goals are to identify all of the approximately 50,000 genes in human deoxyribonucleic acid (DNA) and to determine the sequences of the 3.2 billion base pairs that make up human DNA. The project will also store this information in databases, develop tools for data analysis, and address any ethical, legal, and social issues that may arise.

Makeup of the human chromosome

In order to understand how mammoth an undertaking this ambitious project is, it is necessary to know how genetic instructions are carried on

Words to Know

Chromosome: Structures that organize genetic information in the nucleus of a cell.

DNA (deoxyribonucleic acid): Large, complex molecules found in the nuclei of cells that carry genetic information for an organism's development.

Gene: A segment of a DNA (deoxyribonucleic acid) molecule contained in the nucleus of a cell that acts as a kind of code for the production of some specific protein. Genes carry instructions for the formation, functioning, and transmission of specific traits from one generation to another.

Nucleotide: The basic unit of a nucleic acid. It consists of a simple sugar, a phosphate group, and a nitrogen-containing base. (Pronounced NOO-klee-uh-tide.)

the human chromosome. Humans have forty-six chromosomes, which are coiled structures in the nucleus of a cell that carry DNA. DNA is the genetic material that contains the code for all living things, and it consists of two long chains or strands joined together by chemicals called bases or nucleotides (pronounced NOO-klee-uh-tides), all of which are coiled together into a twisted-ladder shape called a double helix. The bases are considered to be the "rungs" of the twisted ladder. These rungs are made up of only four different types of nucleotides—adenine (A), thymine (T), guanine (G), and cytosine (C)—and are critical to understanding how nature stores and uses a genetic code. The four bases always form a "rung" in pairs, and they always pair up the same way. Scientists know that A always pairs with T, and G always pairs with C. Therefore, each DNA base is like a letter of the alphabet, and a sequence or chain of bases can be thought of as forming a certain message.

The human genome

The human genome, which is the entire collection of genes found in a single set of chromosomes (or all the DNA in an organism), consists of 3.2 billion nucleotide pairs or bases. To get some idea about how much information is packed into a very tiny space, a single large gene may consist of tens of thousands of nucleotides or bases, and a single chromosome may contain as many as one million nucleotide base pairs and four thousand genes. What is most important about these pairs of bases is the particular order of the As, Ts, Gs, and Cs. Their order dictates whether an organism is a human being, a bumblebee, or an apple. Another way of looking at the size of the human genome present in each of our cells is to consider the following phone book analogy. If the DNA sequence of the human genome were compiled in books, 200 volumes the size of the Manhattan telephone book (1,000 pages) would be needed to hold it all. This would take 9.5 years to read aloud without stopping. In actuality, since the human genome is 3.2 billion base pairs long, it will take 3 gigabytes of computer data storage to hold it all.

Two types of maps

In light of the project's main goal—to map the location of all the genes on every chromosome and to determine the exact sequence of nucleotides of the entire genome—two types of maps are being made. One of these is a physical map that measures the distance between two genes in terms of nucleotides. A very detailed physical map is needed before real sequencing can be done. Sequencing is the precise order of the nucleotides. The other map type is called a genetic linkage map and it measures the distance between two genes in terms of how frequently the genes are inherited together. This is important since the closer genes are to each other on a chromosome, the more likely they are to be inherited together.

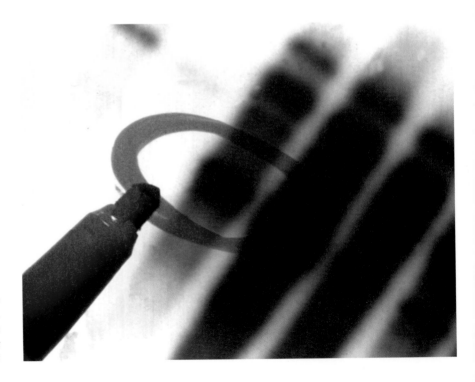

The investigation of genes and DNA sequencing. *(Reproduced by permission of Custom Medical Stock Photo, Inc.)*

Rapid progress

As an international project involving at least eighteen countries, the Human Genome Project was able to make unexpected progress in its early years, and it revised its schedule in 1993 and again in 1998. During December 1999, an international team announced it had achieved a scientific milestone by compiling the entire code of a complete human chromosome for the first time. Researchers chose chromosome 22 because of its relatively small size and its link to many major diseases. The sequence they compiled is over 23 million letters in length and is the longest continuous stretch of DNA ever deciphered and assembled. What was described as the "text" of one chapter of the 23-volume human genetic instruction book was therefore completed. Francis Collins, director of the National Human Genome Research Institute of the National Institutes of Health, said of this success, "To see the entire sequence of a human chromosome for the first time is like seeing an ocean liner emerge out of the fog, when all you've ever seen before were rowboats."

In February 2001, scientists working on the project published the first interpretations of the human genome sequence. Previously, many in the scientific community had believed that the number of human genes totaled about 100,000. But the new findings surprised everyone: both research groups said they could find only about 30,000 or so human genes. This meant that humans have remarkably few genes, not that many more than a fruit fly, which has 13,601 (scientists had decoded this sequence in March 2000). This discovery led scientists to conclude that human complexity does not come from a sheer quantity of genes. Instead, human complexity seems to arise as a result of the structure of the network of different genes, proteins, and groups of proteins and the dynamics of those parts connecting at different times and on different levels.

Private sector competition

The Human Genome Project typically is called "big science," usually referring to a large, complex, and, above all, expensive operation that can only be undertaken by a government. That is why the emergence of private sector (non-governmental) competition in 1998 was such a surprise. During that year, J. Craig Venter, the founder of Celera Genomics, announced that his company planned to sequence the human genome on its own. He said he could achieve this because Celera Genomics was using the largest civilian supercomputer ever made to produce the needed sequences. When Celera began to show real progress, it appeared to many that a race between the public and private sectors would occur. However, once Venter met with Francis Collins, the director of the Human Genome Project, it was agreed that cooperation would achieve more than competition. Therefore, when what was called the "draft sequence" was completed and announced on June 26, 2000, Venter and Collins appeared together and gave the public its first news of this achievement. They stated that the project had compiled what might be called a rough draft of the human genome, having put together a sequence of about 90 percent.

2003 anniversary

Total project completion—meaning that all of the remaining gaps will be closed and its accuracy improved, so that a complete, high-quality reference map is available—is expected in 2003. This will coincide with the fiftieth anniversary of the description of the molecular structure of DNA, first unraveled in 1953 by American molecular biologist James Watson (1928–) and English molecular biologist Francis Crick (1916–). When the genome is completely mapped and fully sequenced in 2003, two years earlier than planned, biologists can for the first time stand back and look at each chromosome as well as the entire human blueprint. They will start to understand how a chromosome is organized, where the genes are located, how they express themselves, how they are duplicated and inherited, and how disease-causing mutations occur. This could lead to the development of new therapies for diseases thought to be incurable as well as to new ways of manipulating DNA.

It also could lead to testing people for "undesirable" genes. However, such a statement leads to all sorts of potential dangers involving ethical and legal matters. Fortunately, such issues have been considered from the beginning. Part of the project's goal is to address these difficult issues of privacy and responsibility, and to use the completely mapped and fully sequenced genome to everyone's benefit.

Future benefits

There is no doubt that the breakthrough in human genome research will mark a revolution in the biology of the twenty-first century. Although we presently have only a glimpse of what the potential benefits of this knowledge may be, there are several good indicators of the fields that may benefit the most. What we have already witnessed is the real beginning of an American biotechnology effort whose genomic research will result in the creation of a multibillion-dollar industry. Many of these new companies that will emerge will develop new DNA-based products and technologies that will improve our health and well-being.

Molecular medicine.   First among these new medical applications might be advances in what is known as molecular medicine. With the knowledge gained from the completion of the Human Genome Project, doctors will be less concerned with the symptoms of a disease or how it shows itself than they will with what actually causes the disease. Detailed genome maps will allow researchers to seek and find the genes that are associated with such diseases as inherited colon and breast cancer and Alzheimer's disease. Not only will doctors be able to diagnose these conditions at a much earlier point, but they will have new types of drugs, as well as new techniques and therapies, that will allow them to cure or even prevent a disease. In the near future, it is expected that doctors will know much earlier whether a person has or is predisposed to getting certain dis-

A researcher loading an automated DNA sequencer at the Joint Genome Institute. *(Reproduced by permission of Photo Researchers, Inc.)*

eases, and to then be able to use certain gene therapies or "custom drugs" to cure these diseases.

New uses for microbes.   Microbes are any forms of life that are too small to be seen without a microscope. Bacteria are the most common form of microbes or microorganisms. In the not-too-distant future, we can expect the knowledge gained from the Human Genome Project to result in science being able to sequence and therefore understand the genomes of bacteria as well as of humans. This, in turn, will result in such highly

Researchers Dr. Nigel Carter and Sheila Clegg studying a FISH micrograph of chromosomes marked to reveal the presence of genes for the Human Genome Project. *(Reproduced by permission of Photo Researchers, Inc.)*

useful applications as energy production, environmental cleanup, toxic waste reduction, and the creation of entirely new industrial processes or ways in which we manufacture things. Eventually, new "biotechnologies" will be developed that will create bacteria that can "digest" waste material of all sorts, produce energy the way plants do, and improve the way industry makes products from food to clothing. Understanding the genetic sequence of bacteria can also show how harmful bacteria work against the body and perhaps how to combat them as well.

Risk assessment. Biologists know already that certain individuals are more susceptible to certain toxic or poisonous agents than others. They know that the cause for these susceptibilities is found in their genetic makeup or in their genes. Understanding the human genome will lead to science being able to identify, ahead of time, those who are at risk in certain environments, and conversely, those who have a stronger, "built-in" resistance. Such knowledge will help to understand and control the cancer risks of people who might be exposed to radiation or similarly dangerous energy-related materials or processes.

Comparative genomics. Comparative genomics means being able to compare the genetic make-up of individuals, groups, and all forms of life. Understanding the human genome and then the genomes of other life forms will enable scientists to better understand human evolution and to learn how people are connected to all other living things. Once researchers discover what the actual genetic "map" is for all major groups of organisms, there will be greater insight into how all life is connected and related.

Forensic science. Forensic science is the use of scientific methods to investigate a crime and to prepare evidence that is presented in court. Any living thing can be easily identified by examining the DNA sequences of the species to which it belongs. Although identifying an individual by its own DNA sequence is less precise, techniques developed during the Human Genome Project have made it presently possible to create a DNA profile of a person with the assurance that there is an extremely small chance that another individual has the exact same "DNA fingerprint." This not only will allow police to identify suspects whose DNA may match evidence left at a crime scene, but it also can, and has, been used to prove others innocent who were wrongly accused or convicted. DNA fingerprinting can identify victims, prove whether a man is the father of a child, and better match organ donors with recipients.

Better crops and animals. A deeper genetic understanding of plants and animals, as well as humans, will allow farmers to develop crops that can better resist disease, insects, and drought. Such "bioengineered" food would enable farmers to use little or no pesticides on the fruit and vegetables we eat, as well as to reduce waste. They could do the same for the animals farmers breed, and could produce healthier, more disease-resistant livestock.

Altogether, the Human Genome Project has already begun to have a major impact on the life sciences and the quality of our lives. Although it has proven to be a highly successful effort and will certainly achieve all of its stated goals, it really marks only the most basic of beginnings in understanding the genetic secrets of life.

[*See also* **Biotechnology; Genetic disorders; Genetic engineering; Genetics**]

Hydrogen

Hydrogen is the simplest of all chemical elements. It is a colorless, odorless, tasteless gas that burns in air to produce water. It has one of the lowest boiling points, −252.9°C (−423.2°F), and freezing points, −259.3°C (−434.7°F), of all elements.

An atom of hydrogen contains one proton and one electron, making it the simplest atom that can be constructed. Because of the one proton in its nucleus, hydrogen is assigned an atomic number of 1. A total of three isotopes of hydrogen exist. Isotopes are forms of an element with the same atomic number but different atomic masses. Protium and deuterium are both stable isotopes, but tritium is radioactive.

Hydrogen isotopes. (Reproduced by permission of The Gale Group.)

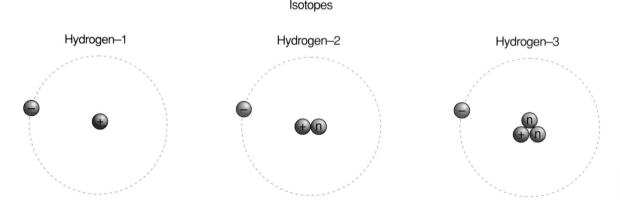

Isotopes

Hydrogen–1　　　　　Hydrogen–2　　　　　Hydrogen–3

The Hydrogen Economy

Some social scientists have called the last century of human history the Fossil Age. That term comes from the fact that humans have relied so heavily on the fossil fuels—coal, oil, and natural gas—for the energy we need to run our societies. What happens when the fossil fuels are exhausted? Where will humans turn for a new supply of energy?

A new generation of scientists is suggesting the use of hydrogen as a future energy source. Hydrogen burns in air or oxygen with a very hot flame that can be used to generate steam, electricity, and other forms of energy. The only product of that reaction is water, a harmless substance that can be released to the environment without danger. In addition, enormous amounts of hydrogen are available from water. Electrolysis can be used to obtain hydrogen from the world's lakes and oceans.

An economy based on hydrogen rather than the fossil fuels faces some serious problems, however. First, hydrogen is a difficult gas with which to work. It catches fire easily and, under certain circumstances, does so explosively. Also, the cost of producing hydrogen by electrolysis is currently much too high to make the gas a useful fuel for everyday purposes.

Of course, once the fossil fuels are no longer available, humans may have no choice but to solve these problems in order to remain a high-energy-use civilization.

Hydrogen is the first element in the periodic table. Its box is situated at the top of Group 1 in the periodic table, but it is not generally considered a member of the alkali family, the other elements that make up Group 1. Its chemical properties are unique among the elements, and it is usually considered to be in a family of its own.

History

Hydrogen was discovered in 1766 by English chemist and physicist Henry Cavendish (1731–1810). It was named by French chemist Antoine-Laurent Lavoisier (1743–1794) from the Greek words for "water-former." Early research on hydrogen was instrumental in revealing the true nature

The Isotopes of Hydrogen

Name	Nucleus	Atomic Number	Atomic Mass	Percent of Hydrogen Atoms
Protium	1 proton	1	1	99.985
Deuterium	1 proton; 1 neutron	1	2	0.015
Tritium	1 proton; 2 neutrons	1	3	trace

of oxidation (burning) and, therefore, was an important first step in the birth of modern chemistry.

Abundance

Hydrogen is by far the most abundant element in the universe. It makes up about 93 percent of all atoms in the universe and about three-quarters of the total mass of the universe. Hydrogen occurs both within stars and in the interstellar space (the space between stars). Within stars, hydrogen is consumed in nuclear reactions by which stars generate their energy.

Hydrogen is much less common as an element on Earth. Its density is so low that it long ago escaped from Earth's gravitational attraction. Hydrogen does occur on Earth in a number of compounds, however, most prominently in water. Water is the most abundant compound on Earth's surface.

Hydrogen also occurs in nearly all organic compounds and constitutes about 61 percent of all the atoms found in the human body. Chemists now believe that hydrogen forms more compounds than any other element, including carbon.

Properties and uses

Hydrogen is a relatively inactive element at room temperature, but it becomes much more active at higher temperatures. For example, it burns in air or pure oxygen with a pale blue, almost invisible flame. It can also be made to react with most elements, both metals and nonmetals. When combined with metals, the compounds formed are called hydrides. Some familiar compounds of hydrogen with nonmetals include ammonia (NH_3), hydrogen sulfide (H_2S), hydrogen chloride (or hydrochloric acid, HCl), hydrogen fluoride (or hydrofluoric acid, H_2F_2), and water (H_2O).

The largest single use of hydrogen is in the production of ammonia. Ammonia, in turn, is used in the production of fertilizers and as a fertilizer itself. It is also a raw material for the production of explosives. Large amounts of hydrogen are also employed in hydrogenation, the process by which hydrogen is reacted with liquid oils to convert them to solid fats. Hydrogen is used in the production of other commercially important chemicals as well, most prominently, hydrogen chloride. Finally, hydrogen acts as a reducing agent in many industrial processes. A reducing agent is a substance that reacts with a metallic ore to convert the ore into a pure metal.

[See also **Periodic table**]

Hydrologic cycle

Hydrologic cycle is the phrase used to describe the continuous circulation of water as it falls from the atmosphere to Earth's surface in the form of precipitation, circulates over and through Earth's surface, then evaporates back to the atmosphere in the form of water vapor to begin the cycle again. The scientific field concerned with the hydrologic cycle, the physical and chemical properties of bodies of water, and the interaction between the waters and other parts of the environment is known as hydrology.

The total amount of water contained in the planet's oceans, lakes, rivers, ice caps, groundwater, and atmosphere is a fixed, global quantity. This amount is about 500 quintillion gallons (1,900 quintillion liters). Scientists believe this total amount has not changed in the last three billion years. Therefore, the hydrologic cycle is said to be constant throughout time.

Earth's water reservoirs and the water cycle

Oceans cover three-quarters of Earth's surface, but contain over 97 percent of all the water on the planet. About 2 percent of the remaining water is frozen in ice caps and glaciers. Less than 1 percent is found underground, in lakes, in rivers, in ponds, and in the atmosphere.

Solar energy causes natural evaporation of water on Earth. Of all the water that evaporates into the atmosphere as water vapor, 84 percent comes from oceans, while 16 percent comes from land. Once in the atmosphere, depending on variations in temperature, water vapor eventually condenses as rain or snow. Of this precipitation, 77 percent falls on oceans, while 23 percent falls on land.

Precipitation that falls on land can follow various paths. A portion runs off into streams and lakes, and another portion soaks into the soil, where it is available for use by plants. A third portion soaks below the root zone and continues moving slowly downward until it enters underground reservoirs of water called groundwater. Groundwater accumulates in aquifers (underground layers of sand, gravel, or spongy rock that collect water) bounded by watertight rock layers. This stored water, which may take several thousand years to accumulate, can be tapped by deep

The hydrologic cycle.
(Reproduced by permission of The Gale Group.)

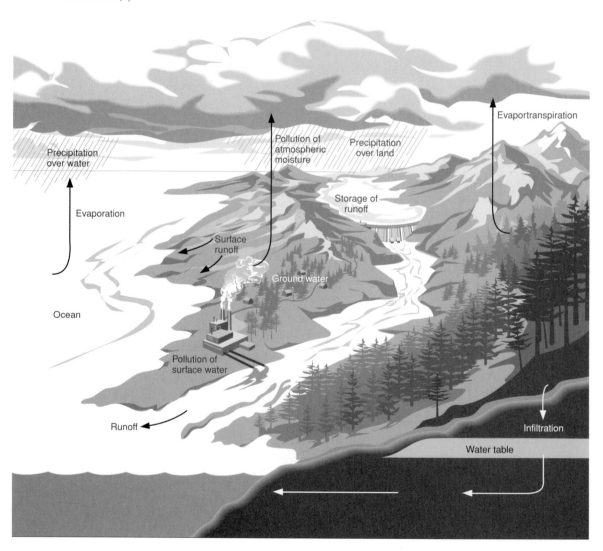

water wells to provide freshwater. It is estimated that the groundwater is equal to 40 times the volume of all the freshwater on Earth's surface.

A plant pulls water from the surrounding soil through its roots and transports it to its stems and leaves. Solar heat on the leaves causes the plant to heat up. The plant naturally cools itself by a process called transpiration, whereby water is eliminated through pores in the leaves (called stomata) in the form of water vapor. This water vapor then moves up into the atmosphere.

A seeping aquifer in Arizona. (Reproduced by permission of JLM Visuals.)

Solar heat also causes the evaporation of water from ground surfaces and from lakes and rivers. The amount of evaporation from these areas is far less than that from the oceans, but the amount of evaporation is balanced as gravity forces water in rivers to flow downhill to empty into the oceans.

An inconsistent cycle

Although the hydrologic cycle is a constant phenomenon, it is not always evident in the same place year after year. If it occurred consistently in all locations, floods and droughts would not exist. However, each year some places on Earth experience more than average rainfall, while other places endure droughts.

[*See also* **Evaporation; Water**]

Ice ages

Ice ages were periods in Earth's history when glaciers and vast ice sheets covered large portions of Earth's surface. Earth's average annual temperature varies constantly from year to year, from decade to decade, and from century to century. During some periods, that average annual temperature has dropped low enough to allow fields of ice to grow and cover large regions of Earth.

The most recent ice age

Over the last 2.5 million years, about two dozen ice ages have occurred. That means that Earth's average annual temperature greatly shifted upwards and downwards about two dozen times during that time. In each case, a period of significant cooling was followed by a period of significant warming—called an interglacial period—after which cooling took place once more.

Scientists know a great deal about the cycle of cooling and warming that has taken place on Earth over the last 125,000 years, the period of the last ice age cycle. They have been able to specify the centuries and decades during which ice sheets began to expand and diminish. For example, the most severe temperatures during the last ice age were recorded about 50,000 years ago. Temperatures then warmed before plunging again about 18,000 years ago.

Clear historical records are available for one of the most severe recent cooling periods, a period now known as the Little Ice Age. This period ran from about the fifteenth to the nineteenth century and caused

Ice Age Refuges

The series of ice ages that occurred between 10,000 and 2,500,000 years ago had a dramatic effect on the climate and life-forms in the tropics. During each glacial period, the tropics became both cooler and drier, turning some areas of tropical rain forest into dry seasonal forest or savanna. However, some areas of forest escaped the dry periods and acted as refuges (protective shelters) for forest plants and animals. During subsequent interglacials, when humid conditions returned to the tropics, the forests expanded and were repopulated by plants and animals from the species-rich refuges.

Ice age refuges correspond to present-day areas of tropical forest that typically receive much rainfall and often contain unusually large numbers of species. The location and extent of the forest refuges have been mapped in both Africa and South America. In the African rain forests, there are three main centers located in Upper Guinea, Cameroon and Gabon, and the eastern rim of the Zaire basin. In the Amazon Basin, more than 20 refuges have been identified for different groups of animals and plants in Peru, Colombia, Venezuela, and Brazil.

widespread crop failure and loss of human life throughout Europe. Since the end of the Little Ice Age, temperatures have continued to move up and down. No one is quite certain whether the last ice age has ended or whether we are still living in it.

Evidence for the ice ages

A great deal of what scientists know about the ice ages they have learned from the study of mountain glaciers. When a glacier moves downward out of its mountain source, it carves out a distinctive shape on the surrounding land. The "footprints" left by ice-age glaciers are comparable to those formed by mountain glaciers.

The transport of materials from one part of Earth's surface to another part is also evidence for ice ages. Rocks and fossils normally found only in one region of Earth may be picked up and moved by ice sheets and deposited elsewhere. Also, moving ice may actually leave scratches on the rock over which it moves, providing further evidence for changes that took place during an ice age.

Causes of the ice ages

Although scientists do not know exactly what causes ice ages or periods of glaciation, they have offered many theories. These theories point to either astronomical (space-based) factors or terrestrial (Earth-based) factors.

Astronomical factors. One of the most obvious astronomical factors is the appearance of sunspots. Sunspots are eruptions that occur on the Sun's surface during which unusually large amounts of solar energy are released. The number of sunspots that occur each year changes according to a fairly regular pattern, reaching a maximum about every 11 years. Some scientists have suggested that the increasing and decreasing amounts of energy sent out during sunspot activity may contribute in some way to the increase and decrease of ice fields on Earth's surface.

Other scientists have pointed to the changes in the geometry of Earth's orbit around the Sun as factors that have led to ice ages. Those

A farm in southern Wisconsin where the stripes formed on the land define a drumlin, which is a hill of glacial origin. *(Reproduced by permission of JLM Visuals.)*

changes have resulted in Earth receiving more or less solar radiation, becoming consequently warmer or cooler. In the 1930s, Serbian mathematician Milutin Milankovitch (1879–1958) proposed a theory to explain such changes. The Milankovitch theory states that three periodic changes in Earth's orbit around the Sun affect the amount of sunlight reaching Earth at different latitudes, leading to ice ages. First, Earth's axis wobbles like a gyroscope, tracing a complete circle every 23,000 years or so. Second, while wobbling, the axis tilts between 22 and 24.5 degrees every 41,000 years. Third, Earth's elliptical orbit pulses, moving outward or inward every 100,000 and 433,000 years.

Terrestrial factors. Changes that take place on Earth itself may also have contributed to the evolution of ice ages. For example, volcanic eruptions can contribute to significant temperature variations. Dust particles thrown into the air during an eruption can reflect sunlight back into space, reducing heat that would otherwise have reached Earth's surface.

A similar factor affecting Earth's annual average temperature might be the impact of meteorites on Earth's surface. If very large meteorites had struck Earth at times in the past, such collisions would have released huge volumes of dust into the atmosphere. The presence of this dust could have also reduced Earth's annual average temperature for an extended period of time.

Whatever the cause of ice ages, it is clear that they can develop as the result of relatively small changes in Earth's average annual temperature. It appears that annual variations of only a few degrees can result in the formation of extensive ice sheets that cover thousands of square miles of Earth's surface.

[*See also* **Geologic time**]

Iceberg

An iceberg is a large mass of free-floating ice that has broken away from a glacier. (Glaciers are flowing masses of ice, created by years of snowfall and cold temperatures.) Beautiful and dangerous, icebergs are carried about the ocean surface until they melt. Most icebergs come from the glaciers of Greenland or from the massive ice sheets of Antarctica.

The process of icebergs breaking off of a glacier is called calving. Icebergs consist of freshwater ice, pieces of debris, and trapped bubbles of air. The combination of ice and air bubbles causes sunlight shining on

▼ **Words to Know**

Calving: Process of iceberg formation in which a glacier flows into the sea and large chunks of glacial ice break free due to stress, pressure, or the forces of waves and tides.

Ice island: Thick slab of floating ice occupying an area as large as 180 square miles (460 square kilometers).

Ice sheet: Glacial ice that covers at least 19,500 square miles (50,000 square kilometers) of land and that flows in all directions, covering and obscuring the landscape below it.

Ice shelf: Section of an ice sheet that extends into the sea a considerable distance and that may be partially afloat.

the icebergs to color the ice spectacular shades of blue, green, and white. Icebergs come in a variety of unusual shapes and sizes, some long and flat, others towering and massive.

An iceberg floats because it is lighter and less dense than the salty seawater, but only a small part of the iceberg is visible above sea level. Typically, about 80 to 90 percent of an iceberg is below sea level. Scientists who study icebergs classify true icebergs as pieces of ice that are higher than 16 feet (5 meters) above sea level and wider than 98 feet (30 meters) at the water line. The largest icebergs can be taller than 230 feet (70 meters) and wider than 738 feet (225 meters). Chunks of ice more massive than this are called ice islands. Ice islands are much more common in the Southern Hemisphere, where they break off from the Antarctic ice sheets.

The life span of an iceberg depends on its size, but is typically about two years in the Northern Hemisphere. Because they are larger, icebergs from Antarctica may last for several more years. The main destructive forces that work against icebergs are wave action and heat. Wave action can break icebergs into smaller pieces. It can also force icebergs to knock into each other, which can fracture them. Relatively warm air and water temperature gradually melt icebergs.

Since icebergs float, they drift with water currents toward the warmer waters near the equator. Icebergs may drift as far as 8.5 miles (14 kilometers) per day. Most icebergs have completely melted by the time they reach about 40 degrees latitude, north and south. There have been rare occasions when icebergs have drifted as far south as the island of Bermuda in the Caribbean, and as far east as the Azores, islands in the Atlantic Ocean off the coast of Spain.

Loss of the *Titanic* to an iceberg

One of the best-known icebergs is the one that struck and sank the ocean liner *Titanic* on her maiden voyage in the spring of 1912. More than 1,500 people lost their lives in that disaster, which occurred near Newfoundland, Canada. As a result of the tragedy, 16 nations agreed to monitor icebergs to protect shipping interests in the North Atlantic sea lanes. Counts of icebergs drifting into the North Atlantic shipping lanes vary from year to year. Some years no icebergs drift into the lanes; other years are marked by hundreds or more. Many ships now carry their own radar equipment to detect icebergs. Some ships even rely on infrared sensors from airplanes and satellites. Sonar is also used to locate icebergs.

Modern iceberg research continues to focus on improving methods of tracking and monitoring icebergs and on learning more about iceberg deterioration. In 1995, a huge iceberg broke free from the Larsen Ice Shelf in Antarctica. Between the fall of 1998 and the spring of 1999, 662 square

An iceberg in Disko Bay on the western coast of Greenland. *(Reproduced by permission of The Stock Market.)*

Hubbard Glacier calving in Alaska. *(Reproduced by permission of Phototake.)*

miles (1,714 square kilometers) of area from the Larsen Ice Shelf calved away. In the fall of 2000, an iceberg measuring 30 by 11.5 miles (48 by 18.5 kilometers) calved from the Ross Ice Shelf in Antarctica. According to some scientists, these highly unusual events could be evidence of global warming.

Some people have proposed towing icebergs to regions of the world that suffer from drought. However, the cost and potential environmental impact of such a project have discouraged any such attempts.

[*See also* **Glaciers**]

Imaginary number

An imaginary number is the square root of a negative real number. (The square root of a number is a second number that, when multiplied by itself, equals the first number.) As an example, $\sqrt{-25}$ is an imaginary number.

The problem with imaginary numbers arises because the square (the result of a number multiplied by itself) of any real number is always a positive number. For example, the square of 5 is 25. But the square of

−5 (−5 × −5) is also 25. What does it mean, then, to say that the square of some number is −25. In other words, what is the answer to the problem $\sqrt{-25} = ?$

As early as the sixteenth century, mathematicians were puzzled by this question. Italian mathematician Girolamo Cardano (1501–1576) is generally regarded as the first person to have studied imaginary numbers. Eventually, a custom developed for using the lowercase letter i to represent the square root of a negative number. Thus $\sqrt{-1} = i$, and $\sqrt{-25} = \sqrt{25} \times \sqrt{-1} = 5i$.

Complex numbers

Imaginary numbers were largely a stepchild in mathematics until the nineteenth century. Then, they were incorporated into another mathematical concept known as complex numbers. A complex number is a number that consists of a real part and an imaginary part. For example, the number $5 + 3i$ is a complex number because it contains a real number (5) and an imaginary number ($3i$). One reason complex numbers are important is that they can be manipulated in ways so as to eliminate the imaginary part.

[*See also* **Complex numbers**]

Immune system

The immune system in a vertebrate (an organism with a backbone) consists of all the cells and tissues that recognize and defend the body against foreign chemicals and organisms. For example, suppose that you receive a cut in your skin. Microorganisms living on your skin are then able to enter your body. They pass into the bloodstream and pass throughout your body. Some of these microorganisms are pathogenic, that is, they may cause illness and even death. As soon as those microorganisms enter your body, its immune system begins to identify them as foreign to your body and to produce defenses that will protect your body against any diseases they may cause.

The study of the immune system is known as immunology and scientists engaged in this field of research are immunologists. Our understanding of the way in which the immune system functions in animals has made possible the prevention of various diseases by means of immunizations. The term immunization refers to the protection of an individual animal against a disease by the introduction of killed or weakened disease-causing organisms into its bloodstream.

▼ Words to Know

Antibody response: The specific immune response that utilizes B cells to kill certain kinds of antigens.

Antigen: Anything that causes an immune response in an animal.

B cell (or B lymphocyte): A lymphocyte that participates in the antibody response.

Helper T cell: A kind of T cell with many functions in the immune system, including the stimulation of the development of B cells.

Histamine: A chemical that causes blood vessels to dilate (become wider), thus increasing blood flow to an area.

Inflammatory response: A nonspecific immune response that causes the release of histamine into an area of injury; also prompts blood flow and immune cell activity at injured sites.

Lymphocyte: White blood cell.

Memory cell: The T and B cells that remain behind after a primary immune response and that respond swiftly to subsequent invasions by the same microorganism.

Nonspecific defenses: Immune responses that generally target all foreign cells.

Phagocytosis: The process by which one cell engulfs another cell.

Plasma cell: A B cell that secretes antibodies.

Proteins: Large molecules that are essential to the structure and functioning of all living cells.

Specific defenses: Immune responses that target specific antigens.

Vaccination: Introducing antigens into the body in order to make memory cells, thereby reducing the likelihood of contracting future diseases caused by those antigens.

Levels of defense

The immune system consists of three levels of response: external barriers; nonspecific responses; and specific responses. Included among the external barriers are the skin and mucous membranes. An animal's skin acts something like a protective wrapping that keeps disease-causing organisms out of the body. Normally, the skin is covered with

Interferons

One of the most exciting new disease-fighting agents is a class of compounds known as interferons. Interferons were first discovered in 1957 by Alick Isaacs and Jean Lindenmann. Isaacs and Lindenmann found that chick embryos injected with the influenza virus released very small amounts of a protein that destroyed the virus. The protein also prevented the growth of any other viruses in the embryos. Isaacs and Lindenmann suggested the name interferon for the protein because of its ability to interfere with viral growth.

Further research showed that interferon was produced within hours of a viral invasion and that most living things (including plants) make the protective protein. Scientists realized that interferons were the first line of defense against viral infection in a cell. They realized that interferons might be effective in treating a number of viral diseases in humans, such as some forms of cancer, genital warts, and multiple sclerosis.

Interferons are classified into two general categories, Type I and Type II. Type I interferons are made by every cell in the body, while Type II interferons are made only by T cells and natural killer (NK) cells. Interferons are also classified according to their molecular structure as alpha, beta, gamma, omega, and tau interferons.

In 1986, interferon-alpha became the first interferon to be approved by the U.S. Food and Drug Administration (FDA) for the treatment of disease, in this case, for hairy-cell leukemia. In 1988, this class of interferons was also approved for the treatment of genital warts, proving effective in nearly 70 percent of patients who do not respond to standard therapies. In that same year, it was approved for treatment of Kaposi's sarcoma, a form of cancer that appears frequently in patients suffering from AIDS.

In 1993, another class of interferon, interferon-gamma, received FDA approval for the treatment of one form of multiple sclerosis characterized by the intermittent appearance and disappearance of symptoms. Interferon-gamma may also have therapeutic value in the treatment of leishmaniasis, a parasitic infection that is prevalent in parts of Africa, North and South America, Europe, and Asia.

untold numbers of organisms, some that are harmless, but others that can cause disease. Virtually none of these organisms has the ability to penetrate the skin. Only when the skin has been broken, as in a cut, can the organisms pass into the body.

Mucous membranes are tissues that excrete a thick, sticky liquid known as mucus. All openings that lead to the interior of the body—the mouth, nose, anal tract, and digestive tract—are covered with mucous membranes. Organisms that try to enter the body through one of these openings tend to become trapped in the mucus, preventing them from entering the body.

Nonspecific immune system.   Organisms that manage to penetrate the body's first line of defense then encounter another hurdle: the body's nonspecific immune system. The term nonspecific means that this line of defense goes into operation whenever *any* kind of foreign material enters the body. The immune systems of animals have developed the ability to tell the difference between its own cells, that is, cells produced by the body, and any other kind of material. The foreign matter might be another kind of organism, such as a bacterium or virus; cells from another animal; or inanimate matter, such as coal dust, pollen, cigarette smoke, or asbestosis fibers. Anything that causes an immune response in an animal is said to be an antigen.

Identification of foreign particles as "not-me" cells is made by a group of white blood cells known lymphocytes. Lymphocytes search out antigens in the bloodstream and destroy them by phagocytosis. Phagocytosis is the process by which one cell surrounds a second cell and engulfs it. Once the foreign cell has been swallowed up by the lymphocyte, it is digested by enzymes released from the lymphocyte.

A colored scanning electron micrograph of a white blood cell. *(Reproduced by permission of Photo Researchers, Inc.)*

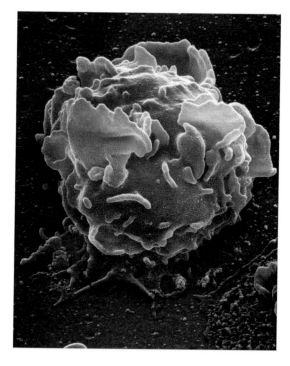

The invasion of antigens can also produce an inflammatory response. Suppose you cut your finger on a tin can. The cut soon becomes red, swollen, and warm. These signs are evidence of the inflammatory response. Injured tissues send out signals to immune system cells, which quickly migrate to the injured area. These immune cells perform different functions. Some destroy bacteria by phagocytosis. Others release enzymes that kill the bacteria. Still other cells release a substance called histamine. Histamine causes blood vessels to dilate (become wider), thus increasing blood flow to the area. All of these activities promote healing in the injured tissue.

Allergic reactions are examples of an inappropriate inflammatory response. When a person is allergic to pollen, the body's immune system is reacting to pollen (a harmless substance) as if it were a bacterium and an immune response is prompted. When pollen is inhaled, it stimulates an inflammatory response in the nasal cavity and sinuses. Histamine is released, which dilates blood vessels and causes large amounts of mucous to be produced, leading to a "runny nose." In addition, histamine stimulates the release of tears and is responsible for the watery eyes and nasal congestion typical of allergies.

To combat these reactions, many people take drugs that deactivate histamine. These drugs, called antihistamines, are available over the counter and by prescription. Some allergic reactions result in the production of large amounts of histamine, which impairs breathing and necessitates prompt emergency care. People prone to these extreme allergic reactions must carry a special syringe with epinephrine (adrenalin), a drug that quickly counteracts this severe respiratory reaction.

Specific immune system. The body's third line of defense against invasion by foreign organisms is the specific immune system. The specific immune system consists of two kinds of lymphocytes known as T lymphocytes and B lymphocytes. The two kinds of cells are sometimes known simply as T cells and B cells. Both kinds of cells are produced in bone marrow. T cells then migrate to the thymus (which gives them the T in their names), where they mature. No one knows where B cells mature.

T cells and B cells differ from nonspecific lymphocytes in that they attack only very specific antigens. For example, the blood and lymph of humans have T cell lymphocytes that specifically target the chicken pox virus, T cell lymphocytes that target the diphtheria virus, and so on. When T cell lymphocytes specific for the chicken pox virus encounters a body cell infected with this virus, the T cell multiplies rapidly and destroys the invading virus.

Two kinds of T cells exist: killer T cells and helper T cells. Killer T cells go directly to the target antigen and attack it. Helper T cells have many different functions, including to help in the development of B cells. Another function is to stimulate the formation of other T cells and the release of various chemicals that aid in the destruction of antigens.

Helper T cells have an especially crucial role in the immune system. Thus, any disease that destroys helper T cells has a devastating effect on the immune system as a whole. HIV (human immunodeficiency virus, which causes AIDS [acquired immunodeficiency syndrome]), for example, infects and kills helper T cells, thus disabling the immune system and leaving the body helpless to stave off infection.

Memory cells. After an invader has been destroyed, some T cells remain behind. These cells are called memory cells. Memory cells give an animal immunity to future attacks by the original invader. Once a person has had chicken pox, memory cells are created. If the person is later exposed to the chicken pox virus again, the virus is quickly destroyed. This secondary immune response, involving memory cells, is much faster than the primary immune response.

The procedure known as vaccination makes use of the above process. Vaccination is the process by which a killed microorganism (or parts thereof) are injected into a person's bloodstream. The presence of these particles prompts the formation of memory cells without a person's having to actually develop the disease.

B cells and the antibody response.   When helper T cells recognize the presence of an invading antigen, they stimulate B cells in the blood and lymph to start reproducing. As the B cells reproduce, they also undergo a change in structure and become known as plasma cells. Those plasma cells then begin to secrete compounds known as antibodies. Antibodies are chemicals released by B cells that attach themselves to the surface of an antigen. The presence of an antibody helps other cells in the immune system recognize the antigen and mark it for destruction.

[*See also* **AIDS (acquired immunodeficiency syndrome); Allergy; Antibody and antigen; Lymphatic system; Vaccine**]

Incandescent light

Incandescent light is given off when an object is heated until it glows. To emit white light, an object must be heated to at least 1,341°F (727°C). White-hot iron in a forge, red lava flowing down a volcano, and the red burners on an electric stove are all examples of incandescence. The most common example of incandescence is the white-hot filament in the lightbulb of an incandescent lamp.

History of incandescent lamps

In 1802, English chemist Humphry Davy (1778–1829) demonstrated that by running electricity through a thin strip of metal, that strip could be heated to temperatures high enough so they would give off light. The strip of metal, called a filament, is resistant to the electricity flowing through it (the thinner the metal, the higher the resistance). The resistance turns the electrical energy into heat, and when the filament becomes white-hot, it gives off light. It incandesces because of the heat. This is the basic principle by which all incandescent lamps work.

↓ Words to Know

Electricity: A form of energy caused by the presence of electrical charges in matter.

Filament: The light source or part of an incandescent lightbulb that is heated until it becomes incandescent.

Incandescence: Glowing due to heat.

Resistance: Anything that causes an opposition to the flow of electricity through a circuit.

In the decades following Davy's demonstration, other scientists and inventors tried to develop workable incandescent lamps. But these lamps were delicate, unreliable, short-lived, and expensive to operate. The lifetime was short because the filaments used would burn up in air. To combat the short lifetime, early developers used thick, low-resistance filaments, but heating them to incandescence required large electrical currents—and generating large currents was costly.

In 1860, English chemist and physicist Joseph Wilson Swan (1828–1914) invented a primitive electric lamp using a filament of carbonized paper in a vacuum glass bulb. In Swan's time, however, it was impossible to make a good enough vacuum. As a result, a wire might be brought to incandescence and produce light for a short time, but it quickly burned up and the light went out. Although the lack of a good vacuum prevented the lamp from working very well, Swan's design helped American inventor Thomas Alva Edison (1847–1931) produce the first practical incandescent lightbulb almost twenty years later.

An important key to Edison's success was that much better vacuums were available by the late 1870s. In addition, Edison knew that the lamp filament should have high, rather than low, resistance. By increasing the resistance, one can reduce the amount of current needed. Increasing the resistance also reduces the amount of energy required to heat the filament to incandescence. After spending fifty thousand dollars in one year's worth of experiments in search of some sort of wire that could be heated to incandescence by an electric current, Edison finally abandoned metal altogether. He then discovered a material that warmed to white heat in a vacuum without melting, evaporating, or breaking—a simple piece of charred cotton thread. On October 21, 1879, Edison first demonstrated in public an incandescent lightbulb—made with his charred cotton thread—that burned continuously for forty hours.

Design

Modern incandescent lamps come in a huge variety of shapes and sizes, but all share the same basic elements. Each is contained by a glass or quartz sphere or envelope. A current enters the lamp through a conductor in an airtight joint or joints. Wires carry the current to the filament, which is held up and away from the bulb by support wires. Changes in the specifics of incandescent lamps have been made to increase efficiency, lifetime, and ease of manufacture.

Although the first common electric lamps were incandescent, many lamps used today are not: Fluorescent lamps, neon signs, and glow-discharge lamps, for example, are not incandescent. Fluorescent lamps are more energy-efficient than incandescent lamps. In the process of radiating light, an incandescent bulb also radiates a huge amount of infrared heat—far more heat than light. The purpose of a lightbulb is to generate light, so the heat is simply wasted energy.

Today, filaments are made of coiled tungsten, a high-resistance material that can be drawn into a wire. It has both a high melting point of 6,120°F (3,382°C) and a low vapor pressure, which keep it from melting or evaporating too quickly. Tungsten also has a higher resistance when it is hot than when it is cold. The filament shape and length are also important to the efficiency of the lamp. Most filaments are coiled, and some are double- and triple-coiled. This allows the filament to lose less heat to the surrounding gas as well as indirectly heating other portions of the filament.

An incandescent lightbulb. *(Reproduced by permission of Phototake.)*

Most lamps have one screw-type base, through which both wires travel to the filament. The base is cemented to the bulb. The bulb may be made from either a regular lead or lime glass or a borosilicate glass that can withstand higher temperatures. Even higher temperatures require the use of quartz, high-silica, or aluminosilicate glasses. Most bulbs are chemically etched inside to diffuse light from the filament.

Placing a coating of powered white silica on the inner surface of the bulb is another method used to diffuse the light.

Lower wattage bulbs have all the atmosphere pumped out, leaving a vacuum. Lights rated at 40 W or more use an inert fill gas that reduces the evaporation of the tungsten filament. Most use argon, with a small percentage of nitrogen to prevent arcing or the sparking produced when the electric current jumps across the space between the lead-in wires. Krypton is also occasionally used because it increases the efficiency of the lamp, but it is also more expensive.

As the bulb ages, the tungsten evaporates. Some of the evaporated tungsten deposits on the inner surface of the bulb, darkening it. (One can tell whether a bulb has a fill gas or is a vacuum bulb by observing the blackening of an old bulb: vacuum bulbs are evenly coated, whereas gas-filled bulbs show blackening concentrated at the uppermost part of the bulb.) As the tungsten evaporates, the filament becomes thinner and its resistance increases. Eventually, a thin spot in the filament causes the filament to break and the bulb "burns out."

Applications

Thousands of different bulbs are available for a myriad of purposes. General service bulbs are made in ranges from 10 W to 1500 W. The higher-wattage bulbs tend to be more efficient at producing light, so it is more energy-efficient to operate one 100-W bulb than two 50-W bulbs. On the other hand, long-life bulbs (which provide longer lifetimes by re-ducing the filament temperature) are less efficient than regular bulbs, but they may be worth using in situations where changing the bulb is a bother or may a hazard.

Spotlights and floodlights generally require accurately positioned, compact filaments. Reflectorized bulbs, such as those used for car head-lights (these are tungsten-halogen bulbs) or overhead downlights (such as those used in track lighting) are made with reflectors built into the bulb: the bulb's shape along one side is designed so that a reflective coating on that inner surface shapes the light into a beam.

[*See also* **Fluorescent light**]

Indicator species

Indicator species are plants and animals that, by their presence, abun-dance, or chemical composition, demonstrate some distinctive aspect of the character or quality of the environment. For example, in areas where metal-rich minerals can be found at the soil surface, indicator species of plants accumulate large concentrations of those minerals in their tissues. Studies have shown levels of nickel as high as 10 percent in the tissues of some varieties of the mustard plant in Russia and as high as 25 percent in the tissues of the *Sebertia acuminata* from the Pacific island of New Caledonia. Similarly, a relative of the mint plant found in parts of Africa has been important in the discovery of copper deposits. This plant grows only in areas that have up to 7 percent copper in their soil.

Ecological significance

More recently, indicator species have begun being used as measures of habitat or ecosystem quality. For example, many species of lichens are very sensitive to toxic gases, such as sulfur dioxide and ozone. These organisms have been monitored in many places to study air pollution. Severe damage to lichens is especially common in cities with chronic air pollution and near large producers of toxic gases, such as metal smelters.

Similarly, certain types of aquatic invertebrates and fish have been surveyed as indicators of water quality and the health of aquatic ecosystems. For example, the presence of "sewage worms" (tubificids) is an

British soldiers (*Cladonia cristatella*), a species of lichen. Because they are sensitive to toxic gases, lichens have been monitored in many places to study air pollution. *(Reproduced by permission of JLM Visuals.)*

almost certain indication that water quality has been degraded by sewage or other oxygen-consuming organic matter. In contrast with most of the animals that live in an unpolluted aquatic environment, tubificid worms can tolerate water almost totally lacking in oxygen.

In some cases, indicator species can be used as measures of the quality of whole habitats or ecosystems. For example, animals with a specialized requirement for old-growth forests can be used as an indicator of the health of that type of ecosystem. Old-growth dependent birds in North America include spotted owls, red-cockaded woodpeckers, and marbled murrelets. If birds such as these thrive in a particular old-growth forest, the forest can be considered to be in good ecological health. On the other hand, if the health of such species begins to decline, the indication is that the habitat itself may be in poor condition.

Many governments are currently conducting research to determine which species of animals or plants can act as sentinels or lookouts for particular environmental contaminants. Through the use of indicator species, it is hoped that potential environmental problems can be identified before they result in irreparable damage.

[*See also* **Pollution**]

Industrial minerals

The term industrial minerals is used to describe naturally occurring nonmetallic minerals that are used extensively in a variety of industrial operations. Some of the minerals commonly included in this category include asbestos, barite, boron compounds, clays, corundum, feldspar, fluorspar, phosphates, potassium salts, sodium chloride, and sulfur.

Asbestos

Asbestos is a general term used for a large group of minerals with similar and complex chemical compositions. These minerals generally contain magnesium, silicon, oxygen, hydrogen, and other elements. The minerals collectively known as asbestos are often subdivided into two smaller groups, the serpentines and amphiboles. All forms of asbestos are best known for an important common property: their resistance to heat and flame. That property is responsible, in fact, for the name asbestos, from the Greek, meaning "unquenchable." Asbestos has been used for thousands of years in the production of heat resistant materials such as lamp wicks.

▼ Words to Know

Abrasive: A finely divided hard material that is used to cut, grind, polish, smooth, or clean the surface of some other material.

Flux: A substance that promotes the joining of two minerals or metals with each other or that prevents the formation of oxides in some kind of industrial process.

Oxide: An inorganic compound whose only negative part is the element oxygen.

Refractory: Any substance with a very high melting point that is able to withstand very high temperatures.

Today, asbestos is used as a reinforcing material in cement, in vinyl floor tiles, in firefighting garments and fireproofing materials, in the manufacture of brake linings and clutch facings, for electrical and heat insulation, and in pressure pipes and ducts.

Prolonged exposure to asbestos fibers can lead to serious respiratory problems, such as asbestosis and/or lung cancer. These diseases usually take many (often 20 or more) years to develop. Thus, men and women who mined the mineral or used it for various construction purposes during the 1940s and 1950s were not aware of the risks to their health until late in their lives. Today, the uses of asbestos in which humans are likely to be exposed to its fibers have largely been discontinued.

Barite

Barite is the name given to a naturally occurring form of barium sulfate ($BaSO_4$). It is commonly found in Canada, Mexico, and the states of Arkansas, Georgia, Missouri, and Nevada. One of the most important uses of barite is in the production of heavy muds that are used in drilling oil and gas wells. It is also used in the manufacture of a number of other commercially important industrial products such as paper coatings, battery plates, paints, linoleum and oilcloth, plastics, lithographic inks, and as a filler in some kinds of textiles. In addition, barium compounds are widely used in medicine to provide the opacity (darkness) that is needed in taking certain kinds of X rays.

Boron compounds

Boron is a nonmetallic element obtained most commonly from naturally occurring minerals known as borates. The borates contain oxygen, hydrogen, sodium, and other elements in addition to boron. Probably the most familiar boron-containing mineral is borax, mined extensively in salt lakes and alkaline soils.

Borax was known in the ancient world and used to make glazes and hard glass. Today, it is still an important ingredient of glassy products, including heat-resistant glass (Pyrex™), glass wool and glass fiber, enamels, and other kinds of ceramic materials. The element boron itself also has a number of interesting uses. For example, it is used in nuclear reactors to absorb excess neutrons, in the manufacture of special-purpose alloys (metal mixtures), in the production of semiconductors, and as a component of rocket propellants.

Corundum

Corundum is a naturally occurring form of aluminum oxide that is found abundantly in Greece and Turkey and in New York State. It is a very hard mineral with a high melting point. In addition, it is relatively inert chemically and does not conduct an electrical current very well.

These properties make corundum highly desirable as a refractory (a substance capable of withstanding very high temperatures) and as an abrasive (a material used for cutting, grinding, and polishing other materials). One of the more common uses of corundum is in the preparation of toothpastes. Its abrasive properties help to keep teeth clean and white.

In its granular form, corundum is known as emery. Many consumers are familiar with emery boards used for filing fingernails. Like corundum, emery is also used in the manufacture of cutting, grinding, and polishing wheels.

Feldspar

The feldspars are a class of minerals known as the aluminum silicates. They all contain aluminum, silicon, and oxygen, as well as other elements, most commonly sodium, potassium, and calcium. In many cases, the name feldspar is reserved for the potassium aluminum silicates. The most important commercial use of feldspar is in the manufacture of pottery, enamel, glass, and ceramic materials. The hardness of the mineral also makes it desirable as an abrasive.

Fluorspar

Fluorspar is a form of calcium fluoride that occurs naturally in many parts of the world, including North America, Mexico, and Europe. The compound gets its name from one of its oldest uses, as a flux. (In Latin, the word *fluor* means "flux.") A flux is a material used in industry to aid in the mixing of other materials or to prevent the formation of oxides during the refining of a metal. For example, fluorspar is often added to an open hearth steel furnace to react with any oxides that might form during that process. The mineral is also used during the smelting of an ore (the removal of a metal from its naturally occurring ore).

Fluorspar is also the principal source of fluorine gas. The mineral is first converted to hydrogen fluoride, which, in turn, is then converted to the element fluorine. Some other uses of fluorspar are in the manufacture of paints and certain types of cement, in the production of emery wheels and carbon electrodes, and as a raw material for phosphors (substances that glow when bombarded with energy, such as the materials used in color television screens).

Phosphates

To a chemist, the term phosphate refers to any chemical compound containing a characteristic grouping of atoms. This grouping contains phosphorus and oxygen atoms (present in the formula PO_4, or in comparable groupings). In the field of industrial minerals, the term most commonly refers to a specific naturally occurring phosphate, calcium phosphate, or phosphate rock.

By far the most important use of phosphate rock is in agriculture, where it is treated to produce fertilizers and animal feeds. Typically, about 80 percent of all the phosphate rock used in the United States goes to one of these agricultural applications.

Phosphate rock is also an important source for the production of other phosphate compounds, such as sodium, potassium, and ammonium phosphate. Each of these compounds, in turn, has a wide array of uses in everyday life. For example, one form of sodium phosphate is a common ingredient in dishwashing detergents. Another, ammonium phosphate, is used to treat cloth to make it fire retardant. And potassium phosphate is used in the preparation of baking powder.

Potassium salts

As with other industrial minerals mentioned here, the term potassium salts applies to a large group of compounds rather than one single compound. Potassium chloride, potassium sulfate, and potassium nitrate are only three of the most common potassium salts used in industry. The first of these, also known as sylvite, can be obtained from salt water or from fossil salt beds. It makes up roughly 1 percent of each deposit, the remainder of the deposit being sodium chloride (halite).

Potassium salts are similar to phosphate rocks in that their primary use is in agriculture, where they are made into fertilizers, and in the chemical industry, where they are converted into other compounds of potassium. Some compounds of potassium have particularly interesting uses. Potassium nitrate, for example, is unstable and is used in the manufacture of explosives, fireworks, and matches.

Sodium chloride

Like potassium chloride, sodium chloride (halite) is found both in sea water and in underground salt mines, where it is left as the result of the evaporation of ancient seas. Sodium chloride has been known to and used by humans for thousands of years. It is best known by its common name of salt, or table salt. By far its most important use is in the manufacture of other industrial chemicals, including sodium hydroxide, hydrochloric acid, chlorine, and metallic sodium. In addition, sodium chloride has many industrial and commercial uses. Among these are the preservation of foods (by salting, pickling, corning, curing, or some other method), road deicing, as an additive for human and other animal foods, in the manufacture of glazes for ceramics, in water softening, and in the manufacture of rubber, metals, textiles, and other commercial products.

Sulfur

Sulfur occurs in its elemental form in large underground deposits from which it is obtained by traditional mining processes or, more commonly, by the Frasch process. In the Frasch process, superheated water is forced down a pipe that has been sunk into a sulfur deposit. The heated water melts the sulfur, which is then forced up a second pipe to Earth's surface.

The vast majority of sulfur is used to manufacture a single compound, sulfuric acid. Sulfuric acid consistently ranks number one in the United States as the chemical produced in largest quantity. It has a very large number of uses, including the manufacture of fertilizers, the refining of petroleum, the pickling of steel (the removal of oxides from the metal's surface), and the preparation of detergents, explosives, and synthetic fibers.

A significant amount of sulfur is also used to produce sulfur dioxide gas (actually an intermediary in the manufacture of sulfuric acid). Sulfur dioxide, in turn, is used extensively in the pulp and paper industry, as a refrigerant, and in the purification of sugar and the bleaching of paper and other products.

Some sulfur is refined after being mined and then used in its elemental form. This sulfur finds application in the vulcanization of rubber, as an insecticide or fungicide, and in the preparation of various chemicals and pharmaceuticals. (Vulcanization is a chemical treatment process that gives rubber its elasticity and strength.)

[See also **Potassium; Sodium chloride; Sulfur**]

Industrial Revolution

Industrial Revolution is the name given to changes that took place in Great Britain during the period from roughly 1730 to 1850. It was originated by German author Friedrich Engels (1820–1895) in 1844. In general, those changes involved the transformation of Great Britain from a largely agrarian (farming) society to one dominated by industry. These changes later spread to other countries, transforming almost all the world.

The Industrial Revolution involved some of the most profound changes in human society in history. Most of the vast array of changes took place in one of three major economic industries: textiles, iron and steel, and transportation. These changes had far-reaching effects on the British economy and social system.

The textile industry

Prior to the mid-eighteenth century, the manufacture of textiles (woven cloth or fabric) in Great Britain (and the rest of the world) took place almost exclusively in private homes. Families would obtain thread from wholesale outlets and then produce cloth by hand in their own houses. Beginning in the 1730s, however, a number of inventors began to develop machines that took over one or more of the previous hand-knitting operations.

In 1733, John Kay (1704–1764) invented the first fly shuttle. This machine consisted of a large frame to which was suspended a series of threads. A shuttle, a device that carried more thread, was then passed through the suspended threads, weaving a piece of cloth. Workers became so proficient with the machine that they could literally make the shuttle "fly" through the thread framework.

Over the next half century, other machines were developed that further mechanized the weaving of cloth. These included the spinning jenny (invented by James Hargreaves in 1764), the water frame (Richard Arkwright, 1769), the spinning mule (Samuel Crompton, 1779), the power loom (Edmund Cartwright, 1785), and the cotton gin (Eli Whitney, 1792).

At least as important as the invention of individual machines was the organization of industrial operations for their use. Large factories, powered by steam or water, sprang up throughout the nation for the manufacture of cloth and clothing.

The development of new technology in the textile industry had a ripple effect on society. As cloth and clothing became more readily available at more modest prices, the demand for such articles increased. This increase in demand had the further effect of encouraging the expansion of business and the search for even more efficient forms of technology.

Iron and steel manufacture

One factor contributing to the development of industry in Great Britain was that nation's large supply of coal and iron ore. For many centuries, the British had converted their iron ores to iron and steel by heating the raw material with charcoal, made from trees. By the mid-eighteenth century, however, the nation's timber supply had largely been used up. Iron and steel manufacturers were forced to look elsewhere for a fuel to use in treating iron ores.

The fuel they found was coal. When coal is heated in the absence of air it turns into coke. Coke proved to be a far superior material for the conversion of iron ore to iron and steel. It was eventually cheaper to produce than charcoal and it could be packed more tightly into a blast furnace, allowing the heating of a larger volume of iron.

The conversion of the iron and steel business from charcoal to coke was accompanied, however, by a number of new technical problems. These, in turn, encouraged the development of even more new inventions. For example, the use of coke in the smelting (melting or fusing) of iron ores required a more intense flow of air through the furnace. Fortunately, the steam engine that had been invented by Scottish engineer James Watt (1736–1819) in 1763 provided the means for solving this problem. The Watt steam engine was also employed in the mining of coal, where it was used to remove water that collected within most mines.

Transportation

For nearly half a century, James Watt's steam engine was so bulky and heavy that it was used only as a stationary power source. The first forms of transport that made use of steam power were developed not in Great Britain, but in France and the United States. In those two nations, inventors constructed the first ships powered by steam engines. In the United States, Robert Fulton's steam ship *Clermont,* built in 1807, was among these early successes.

During the first two decades of the nineteenth century, a handful of British inventors devised carriage-type vehicles powered by steam engines. In 1803, Richard Trevithick (1771–1833) built a "steam carriage" which he carried passengers through the streets of London. A year later,

Industrial
Revolution

The Corliss steam engine was a symbol of the nineteenth-century belief in progress and industry. The 700-ton (636 metric ton), 1,400-to-1,600-horsepower engine powered all the exhibits at the Centennial Exhibition in Philadelphia, Pennsylvania, in 1876. *(Reproduced courtesy of the Library of Congress.)*

one of his steam-powered locomotives pulled a load of 10 tons for a distance of almost 10 miles (16 kilometers) at a speed of about 5 miles (8 kilometers) per hour.

Effects of the Industrial Revolution

The Industrial Revolution brought about dramatic changes in nearly every aspect of British society. With the growth of factories, for example, people were drawn to metropolitan centers. The number of cities with populations of more than 20,000 in England and Wales rose from 12 in 1800 to nearly 200 in 1900.

Technological change also made possible the growth of capitalism. Factory owners and others who controlled the means of production rapidly became very rich. In the years between 1800 and 1900, the total national income in Great Britain increased by a factor of ten.

However, working conditions in the factories were poor. Men, women, and children alike were employed at extremely low wages in crowded, unhealthy, and dangerous environments. Workers were often able to afford no more than the simplest housing, resulting in the rise of urban slums.

These conditions soon led to actions to protect workers. Laws were passed requiring safety standards in factories, setting minimum age limits for young workers, establishing schools for children whose parents both worked, and creating other standards for the protection of workers. Workers then began to establish the first labor unions to protect their own interests; as a group they had more power when bargaining with their employers over wages and working conditions.

Infrared astronomy

Infrared astronomy involves the use of special telescopes that detect electromagnetic radiation (radiation that transmits energy through the interaction of electricity and magnetism) at infrared wavelengths. The recent development of this technology has led to the discovery of many new stars, galaxies, asteroids, and quasars.

Electromagnetic spectrum

Light is a form of electromagnetic radiation. The different colors of light that our eyes can detect correspond to different wavelengths of light. Red light has the longest wavelength; violet has the shortest. Orange, yel-

Words to Know

Dwarf galaxy: An unusually small, faint group of stars.

Electromagnetic radiation: Radiation that transmits energy through the interaction of electricity and magnetism.

Infrared detector: An electronic device for sensing infrared light.

Infrared light: Portion of the electromagnetic spectrum with wavelengths slightly longer than optical light that takes the form of heat.

Optical (visible) light: Portion of the electromagnetic spectrum that we can detect with our eyes.

Quasars: Extremely bright, starlike sources of radio waves that are the oldest known objects in the universe.

Redshift: Shift of an object's light spectrum toward the red-end of the visible light range—an indication that the object is moving away from the observer.

Stellar nurseries: Areas within glowing clouds of gas and dust where new stars are formed.

low, green, blue, and indigo are in between. Infrared light, ultraviolet light, radio waves, microwaves, and gamma rays are all forms of electromagnetic radiation, but they differ in wavelength and frequency. Infrared light has slightly longer wavelengths than red light. Our eyes cannot detect infrared light, but we can feel it as heat.

Infrared telescopes

Two types of infrared telescopes exist: those on the ground and those carried into space by satellites. The use of ground-based telescopes is somewhat limited because carbon dioxide and water in the atmosphere absorb much of the incoming infrared radiation. The best observations are made at high altitudes in areas with dry climates. Since infrared telescopes are not affected by light, they can be used during the day as well as at night.

Space-based infrared telescopes pick up much of the infrared radiation that is blocked by Earth's atmosphere. In the early 1980s, an international group made up of the United States, England, and the Netherlands launched the Infrared Astronomical Satellite (IRAS). Before running out of liquid helium (which the satellite used to cool its infrared detectors) in 1983, IRAS uncovered never-before-seen parts of the Milky Way, the galaxy that's home to our solar system.

In 1995, the European Space Agency launched the Infrared Space Observatory (ISO), an astronomical satellite. Before it ran out of liquid helium in 1998, the ISO discovered protostars, planet-forming nebula around dying stars, and water throughout the universe (including in the gas giants like the planets Saturn and Uranus).

In mid-2002, the National Aeronautics and Space Administration (NASA) plans to launch the Space Infrared Telescope Facility (SIRTF), which will see infrared radiation and peer through the veil of gas and dust that obscures most of the universe from view. It will be the most sensitive instrument ever to look at the infrared spectrum in the universe. SIRTF researchers will study massive black holes, young dusty star systems, and the evolution of galaxies up to 12 billion light-years away.

The United Kingdom Infrared Telescope atop the dormant volcano Mauna Kea in Hawaii. Because infrared light is absorbed by carbon dioxide and water vapor, astronomers use this dry, high-altitude site to minimize the infrared light lost to surrounding air. *(Reproduced by permission of Photo Researchers, Inc.)*

Discoveries with infrared telescopes

Infrared telescopes have helped astronomers find where new stars are forming, areas known as stellar nurseries. A star forms from a collapsing cloud of gas and dust. Forming and newly formed stars are still enshrouded by a cocoon of dust that blocks optical light. Thus infrared astronomers can more easily probe these stellar nurseries than optical astronomers can. The view of the center of our galaxy is also blocked by large amounts of interstellar dust. The galactic center is more easily seen by infrared than by optical astronomers.

With the aid of infrared telescopes, astronomers have also located a number of new galaxies, many too far away to be seen by visible light. Some of these are dwarf galaxies, which are more plentiful—but contain fewer stars—than visible galaxies. The discovery of these infrared dwarf galaxies has led to the theory that they once dominated the universe and then came together over time to form visible galaxies, such as the Milky Way.

With the growing use of infrared astronomy, scientists have learned that galaxies contain many more stars than had ever been imagined. Infrared telescopes can detect radiation from relatively cool stars, which give off no visible light. Many of these stars are the size of the Sun. These discoveries have drastically changed scientists' calculations of the total mass in the universe.

Infrared detectors have also been used to observe far-away objects such as quasars. Quasars have large redshifts, which indicate that they are moving away from Earth at high speeds. In a redshifted object, the waves of radiation are lengthened and shifted toward the red end of the spectrum. Since the redshift of quasars is so great, their visible light gets stretched into infrared wavelengths. While these infrared wavelengths are undetectable with optical telescopes, they are easily viewed with infrared telescopes.

[See also **Electromagnetic spectrum; Galaxy; Spectroscopy; Star; Starburst galaxy**]

Insects

Insects are invertebrates in the class *Insecta*, which contains 28 living orders. The animals that make up this class have a number of distinctive features. Their adult bodies are typically divided into three parts, known as the head, thorax, and abdomen. In addition, they have three pairs of segmented legs attached to the thorax and one pair of antennae. Members of the subclass *Pterygota* have two pairs of wings as adults. By contrast, some relatively primitive members of the subclass *Apterygota* are wingless.

Taxonomists (scientists who classify organisms) have recognized more than one million species of insects, more than any other group of organisms. In addition, scientists believe that tens of millions of species of insects remain undiscovered. Currently, scientists estimate that as many as 30 million species of insects inhabit Earth; most of these are thought to be beetles. In fact, all of the insect orders are poorly known. Most of the undiscovered species of insects occur in tropical rain forests, especially in the upper parts of the forest known as the canopy.

Globally, the insects exploit a remarkable diversity of habitats. They are ecologically important as herbivores (plant-eaters), predators (meat-eaters who hunt their prey), parasites (who feed on living organisms), and scavengers (who feed on dead organisms). As a result of these attributes, insects are considered to be one of the most successful group of organisms on Earth, if not the most successful.

External and internal features of a generalized insect. *(Reproduced by permission of The Gale Group.)*

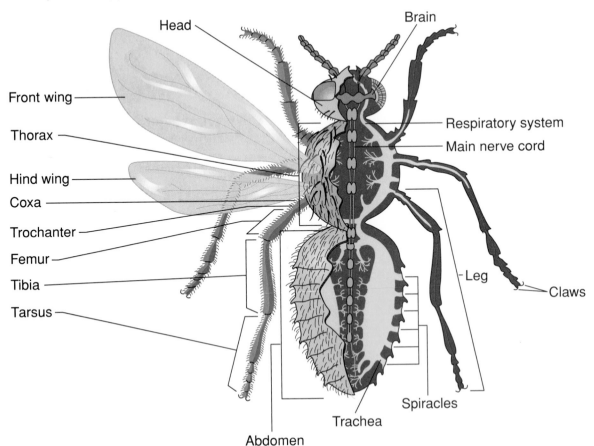

▼ True Bugs

To a biologist, the term bug has a very special meaning. It does not refer to just any insect, as it may when nonscientists use the term. True bugs are members of the order Hemiptera. The order consists of about 35,000 widely different species. Examples of terrestrial (land-living) bugs living in North America are lice, aphids, bedbugs, stink bugs, plant and leaf bugs, assassin bugs, ambush bugs, seed bugs, lace bugs, and squash bugs. Examples of aquatic bugs are water boatmen, backswimmers, giant water bugs, water scorpions, and water striders.

Bugs have two sets of wings although in some species, the wings are greatly reduced in size and the animals cannot fly. The mouthparts of bugs are adapted for piercing and sucking. Most bugs use these mouthparts to feed on plant juices. A few are parasites of vertebrates, living on the animal's surface and feeding on its blood.

Most bugs have long, segmented antennae. They tend to have well-developed compound eyes, although some species have several simple eyes as well. Many species of bugs have glands that give off a strongly scented, distasteful odor when the insect is disturbed. The common name of one species, the stink bug, is evidence for this fact.

Some species of true bugs are brightly and boldly colored. In most cases, these bugs feed on plants that contain poisonous chemicals that also occur in the bugs. These chemicals cause the insects to taste bad, providing protection for them from predators. The bright coloring provides a warning to predators that their prey not only look beautiful, but also taste bad.

While many bugs attack agricultural crops and cause economic harm to humans, a few are health hazards also. Bed bugs, for example, feed by sucking the blood of birds or mammals, including humans. Although their bites are irritating, they do not carry disease. By contrast, the Central and South American bugs sometimes known as kissing bugs are known to transmit the parasitic protozoan that causes Chagas' disease. Chagas' disease is characterized by recurring fever and may cause serious damage to the heart muscles.

Life cycles

Insects have a complex life cycle that consists of a series of intricate transformations called metamorphoses. At each stage of its life cycle, an insect is likely to have very different body shapes, functions, and behaviors. The most complicated life cycles have four stages: egg, larva, pupa, and adult. Examples of insect orders with this life cycle include butterflies, moths, and true flies. Other orders of insects have a less complex development with only three stages: egg, nymph, and adult. Insect orders with this life cycle include the relatively primitive springtails and true bugs.

Most insects are nonsocial. However, some species have developed remarkably complex social behaviors, with large groups of closely related individuals living together and caring for the eggs and young of the group. In such groups, the young are usually the offspring of a single female, known as the queen. This social system is most common in bees, wasps, ants, and termites.

Insects and humans

A few species of insects are useful to humans. For example, we obtain honey from bees and silk from silk worms. Some insects, however, are detrimental because they transmit human diseases. For example, malaria, yellow fever, sleeping sickness, and certain types of encephalitis are caused by microorganisms. These microorganisms are transmitted by certain species of biting flies, especially mosquitoes. When one of these insects bites a human, it may ingest a disease-causing microorganism in the blood it drinks. When the insect bites a second person, it may then transfer that microorganism—along with the disease it causes—to its second victim.

Other insects eat the leaves off trees and thereby cause substantial damage to commercial timber stands and to shade trees. Insects may also defoliate (remove the leaves from) agricultural plants, or they may feed on unharvested or stored grains, thus causing great economic losses. Some insects, particularly termites, cause enormous damage to wood, literally eating buildings constructed of that material. Pesticides—chemicals that are toxic to insects—are sometimes used to control the populations of insects that are regarded as major pests.

[*See also* **Agrochemicals; Butterflies; Cockroaches**]

Integrated circuit

An integrated circuit is a single, miniature circuit with many electronically connected components etched onto a small piece of silicon or some other semiconductive material. (A semiconductor is a nonmetallic mate-

▼ Words to Know

Capacitor: Device in an electric circuit that temporarily stores electrical charge.

Circuit: The complete closed path through which an electric current travels.

Electric circuit: The closed path through which an electric current (flow of electrons) travels.

Microchip: Another name for an integrated circuit.

Resistor: Device in an electric circuit that controls current by providing resistance.

Semiconductor: Substance, such as silicon or germanium, that can conduct an electric current, but does so rather poorly.

Transistor: Semiconductor device capable of amplifying and switching electrical signals.

rial that can conduct an electric current, but does so rather poorly.) Integrated circuits are more commonly known as microchips.

The components etched onto an microchip include transistors, capacitors, and resistors. A transistor is a device capable of amplifying and switching electrical signals. A capacitor temporarily stores electrical charges, while a resistor controls current by providing resistance. The complete closed path through which an electric current travels is called a circuit.

The invention of the transistor in 1948 eliminated the need for bulky vacuum tubes in computers, televisions, and other electronic devices. As other components were also reduced in size, engineers were able to design smaller and increasingly complex electronic circuits. However, the transistors and other parts of the circuit were made separately and then had to be wired together—a difficult task that became even more difficult as circuit components became tinier and more numerous. Circuit failures often occurred when the wire connections broke. The idea of manufacturing an electronic circuit with multiple transistors as a single, solid unit arose as a way to solve this problem.

In the late 1950s, two engineers—Jack Kilby (1923–) of Texas Instruments and Robert Noyce (1927–1990) of Fairchild Semiconductor— began wrestling with the circuit problem. Independently, the two men developed similar devices. Kilby's circuit, however, was made of germanium and was less efficient and hard to produce. Noyce's was constructed of silicon. Transistors were etched onto the silicon chips, thus eliminating the need for costly wire connections. The reduction in size of the circuit components brought about an increase in the speed of their operation.

At first, only a few transistors could be etched on a microchip. By 1964, the number grew to 10. Ten years later, the number had reached 32,000. Today, a chip can carry more than 1,000,000.

The integrated circuit completely revolutionized the electronics industry. The individual transistor, like the vacuum tube before it, became obsolete. The integrated circuit was much smaller, more reliable, cheaper, and far more powerful. It made possible the development of the microprocessor and the personal computer, pocket calculators, microwave ovens, digital watches, and missile guidance systems. And the revolution

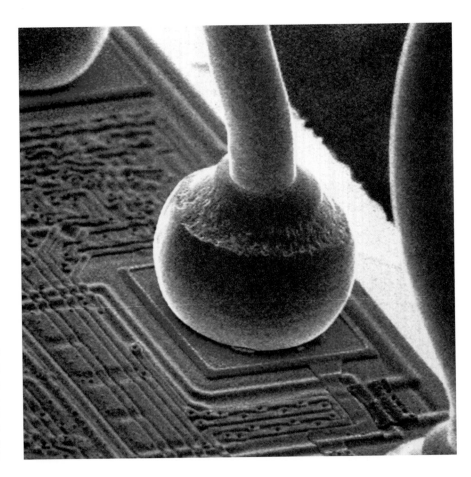

A colored scanning electron micrograph of the end of a gold micro-wire bonded to the silicon chip that houses an integrated circuit. The photo is magnified 280 times. *(Reproduced by permission of Photo Researchers, Inc.)*

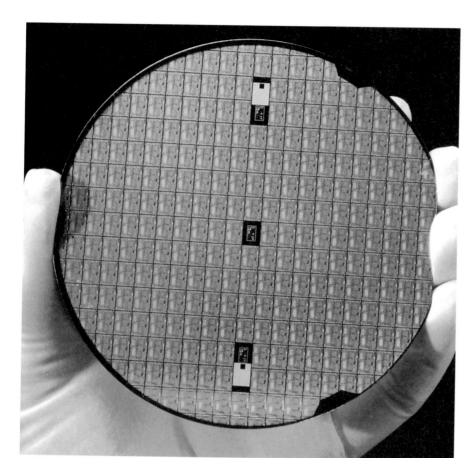

A circular wafer of silicon carrying numerous individual intergrated circuits. Multiple circuits are formed on one silicon base and later cut from it. *(Reproduced by permission of Photo Researchers, Inc.)*

continues to the present, as integrated circuits can be found in almost all electronic devices.

[*See also* **Diode; Electric circuit; Electronics; Transistor**]

Integumentary system

The human integumentary system is made up of the skin, hair, nails, and associated glands. Its main function is to protect the body. It prevents excessive water loss, keeps out microorganisms that could cause illness, and shields the underlying tissues from external damage.

The skin helps to regulate body temperature. If heat builds up in the body, sweat glands in the skin produce sweat, which evaporates and cools the skin. When the body overheats, blood vessels in the skin expand and bring more warm blood to the surface, where it cools. When the body

↓ **Words to Know**

Calluses: Abnormal thickenings of the epidermis.

Dermis: Thicker layer of skin lying below the epidermis.

Epidermis: Thinner outermost layer of the skin.

Keratin: Insoluble protein found in hair, nails, and skin.

Melanin: Brown-black pigment found in skin and hair.

Subcutaneous layer: Layer of fatty tissue found beneath the skin.

gets too cold, the blood vessels in the skin contract, leaving less blood at the body surface, and its heat is conserved.

In addition to temperature regulation, the skin serves as a minor excretory organ. Sweat removes small amounts of wastes produced by the body. These wastes include salts and urea (a chemical compound of carbon, hydrogen, nitrogen, and oxygen). The skin also functions as a sense organ since it contains millions of nerve endings that detect heat, cold, pain, and pressure. Finally, the skin produces vitamin D in the presence of sunlight and renews and repairs damage to itself.

In an adult, the skin covers about 21.5 square feet (2 square meters), and weighs about 11 pounds (5 kilograms). Depending on location, the skin ranges from 0.02 to 0.16 inch (0.5 to 4.0 millimeters) thick. Its two principal parts are the epidermis (the outer layer) and dermis (thicker inner layer). A subcutaneous (under the skin) layer of adipose or fatty tissue is found below the dermis. Fibers from the dermis attach the skin to the subcutaneous layer, and the underlying tissues and organs also connect to the subcutaneous layer.

The epidermis

Ninety percent of the epidermis, including the outer layers, contain cells that produce keratin, a protein that helps waterproof and protect the skin. Keratin is also the major protein found in nails and hair. Pigment cells called melanocytes produce melanin, a brown-black pigment that gives color to the skin and absorbs and reflects the Sun's harmful ultraviolet rays.

In most areas of the body, the epidermis consists of four layers. The epidermis on the soles of the feet and palms of the hands has five layers, since these areas receive a lot of friction. Calluses, abnormal thickenings of the epidermis, can occur on any area of the skin where there is irritation or constant pressure. The uppermost layer of the epidermis consists of about 25 rows of flat dead cells that contain keratin. At the skin surface, dead cells are constantly shed.

The dermis

The dermis is thick in the palms and soles, but very thin in other places, such as the eyelids. The dermis is composed of connective tissue that contains protein fibers (called collagen) and elastic fibers. It also contains blood and lymph vessels, sensory nerves, and glands. Sweat glands are embedded in the deep layers of the dermis. Their ducts pass through the epidermis to the outside and open on the skin surface through pores.

Hair and hair roots also originate in the dermis. Hair shafts (containing the bulb of hair) extend from the hair root through the skin layers to the surface. Attached to the hair shaft is a sebaceous gland, which produces an oily substance called sebum. Sebum softens the hair and prevents it from drying. If sebum blocks up a sebaceous gland, a whitehead appears on the skin. A blackhead results if the material oxidizes and dries. Acne is caused by infections of the sebaceous glands. When this occurs, the skin breaks out in pimples and can become scarred.

A cross section of the skin. Structures used for sensing are labeled on the right. *(Reproduced by permission of The Gale Group.)*

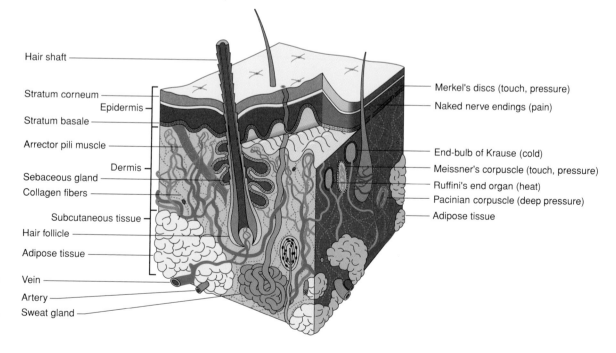

Hair shaft

Stratum corneum
Epidermis
Stratum basale

Arrector pili muscle
Dermis
Sebaceous gland
Collagen fibers

Subcutaneous tissue
Hair follicle

Adipose tissue

Vein
Artery
Sweat gland

Merkel's discs (touch, pressure)
Naked nerve endings (pain)

End-bulb of Krause (cold)
Meissner's corpuscle (touch, pressure)
Ruffini's end organ (heat)
Pacinian corpuscle (deep pressure)
Adipose tissue

Nerves in the dermis carry impulses to and from hair muscles, sweat glands, and blood vessels. Bare nerve endings throughout the skin report information to the brain about temperature change (both heat and cold), pressure, and pain.

The Sun and skin

Some skin disorders result from overexposure to the ultraviolet (UV) rays in sunlight. UV rays damage skin cells, blood vessels, and other dermal structures. At first, overexposure to sunlight results in injury known as sunburn. Continual overexposure leads to leathery skin, wrinkles, and discoloration. It can eventually lead to skin cancer, regardless of the amount of melanin in the epidermis. There can be a 10- to 20-year delay between exposure to sunlight and the development of skin cancer.

[*See also* **Cancer**]

Interference

Interference is the interaction of two or more waves. Wave motion is a common phenomenon in everyday life. Light and sound, for example, are transmitted by waves. In addition, waves can often be seen on lakes, ponds, and other bodies of water.

All waves have high points, called crests, and low points, called troughs (pronounced trawfs). Suppose that two or more waves are generated at the same time, as shown in the accompanying photograph. Here, water waves are spreading out from the point where pebbles have been dropped into a pond. You can see how the waves overlap each other at various points on the surface of the water. This overlapping effect is interference.

Constructive and destructive interference

In general, waves can interfere with each other in one of two ways: constructively or destructively. When the crests of two waves and the troughs of two waves arrive at a given spot at the same time, their effects are added to each other. The result is constructive interference. When the crest of one wave and the trough of a second wave arrive at the same time, their effects cancel each other out. The result is destructive interference.

Interference of sound waves. Constructive and destructive interference can be detected by the intensity of the result. For example, suppose that two sound waves interfere with each other constructively. In that case, the sound is louder than is the case for either wave individually. If the two sound waves interfere destructively, the sound is more quiet than with either wave individually.

Interference of light waves. Interference of light waves has been studied for many years. It was first described in 1801 by English physician and physicist (one who studies the science of matter and energy) Thomas Young (1773–1829). Young found that light waves can be made to interfere in such a way as to produce bright and dark bands called fringes.

Interference also accounts for the range of colors (called a rainbow or spectrum) sometimes produced by reflected light. When white light from the Sun reflects off a thin film of oil, interference may occur. Light of some colors is reflected off the top of the film. Light of other colors is reflected off the bottom of the film. The two sets of reflected light interfere with each other either constructively or destructively. Constructive interference results in the production of bright colors of different shades. Destructive interference produces dark bands with no color.

Applications

Modern technology makes use of interference in many ways. Some experimental automobile mufflers listen for the sound wave produced in

Interference patterns created by the waves from several fallen drops of water. *(Reproduced by permission of Photo Researchers, Inc.)*

the exhaust system. The muffler then produces another sound wave that is out of phase with the exhaust sound. The two waves interfere destructively, canceling the noise that would otherwise be produced by the exhaust system.

The oil film phenomenon described earlier is used for filtering light. Precise coatings on optical lenses in binoculars or cameras, astronaut's visors, or even sun glasses cause destructive interference that eliminates certain unwanted colors or stray reflections.

[*See also* **Diffraction; Interferometry; Wave motion**]

Interferometry

Interferometry is the process of making measurements by allowing sound, light, or other kinds of waves to interfere with each other. Interferometry is used for a large variety of purposes, such as studying the velocity of sound in a fluid, locating the position and properties of objects in space, determining the size and properties of objects without actually touching or otherwise disturbing them, and visualizing processes such as crystal growth, combustion (burning), diffusion (spreading), and shock wave motion.

Principle of the interferometer

The interferometer was invented by German American physicist Albert A. Michelson (1852–1931) around 1881. The major features of Michelson's instrument are shown in Figure 1. Light from the source enters the interferometer along one arm and strikes a half-mirrored glass called a beam splitter. The light is split into two equal parts at the beam splitter. The first half reflects off the beam splitter and travels to mirror #1. The second half passes through the beam splitter to mirror #2.

The first beam of light reflects off mirror #1, passes back through the beam splitter, and continues to the detector. Meanwhile, the second beam reflects off mirror #2, returns to the beam splitter, and is also reflected to the detector.

What happens at the detector depends on the paths taken by the two beams. If they have both traveled exactly the same length, they will interfere with each other constructively. But if the distance taken by the two beams is different, an interference pattern will be formed. The kind of pattern produced, then, depends on the difference between the paths taken by the two beams of light.

Words to Know

Beam splitter: A sheet of glass or plastic specially coated to reflect part of a beam of light and transmit the remainder.

Interference: The interaction of two or more waves.

Velocity: The rate at which the position of an object changes with time, including both the speed and the direction.

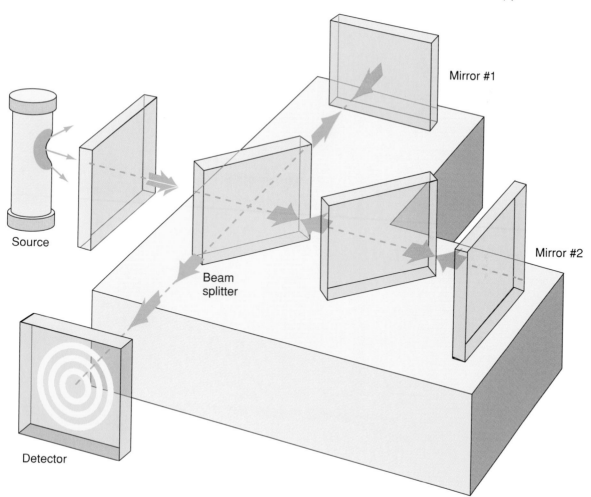

Figure 1. The Michelson interferometer. *(Reproduced by permission of The Gale Group.)*

Mirror #1

Mirror #2

Source

Beam splitter

Detector

Variations on the Michelson interferometer

In the hundred years since Michelson invented the interferometer, scientists have devised a number of variations on the original instrument. Most of these variations were designed to make special kinds of measurements. One example is the interferometer invented in 1891 by L. Mach and L. Zehnder. A top view of this instrument is shown in Figure 2.

Light leaves the source and is divided into two beams by beam splitter #1. One beam travels toward mirror #1 and is reflected toward beam splitter #2. The other beam travels toward mirror #2, where it is also reflected toward beam splitter #2. The two beams are then combined at beam splitter #2 and transmitted to the detector, where an interference pattern is produced. The Mach-Zehnder two-beam interferometer is used for observing gas flows and shock waves and for optical testing. It has also been used to obtain interference fringes of electrons that exhibit wave-like behavior.

[*See also* **Light**]

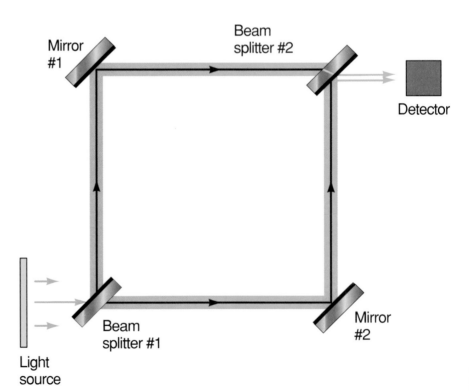

Figure 2. Top view of the interferometer introduced by Mach and Zehnder. *(Reproduced by permission of The Gale Group.)*

Internal-combustion engine

The invention and development of the internal-combustion engine in the nineteenth century has had a profound impact on human life. The internal-combustion engine offers a relatively small, lightweight source for the amount of power it produces. Harnessing that power has made possible practical machines ranging from the smallest model airplane to the largest truck. Lawnmowers, chainsaws, and electric generators also may use internal-combustion engines. An important device based on the internal-combustion engine is the automobile.

In all internal-combustion engines, however, the basic principles remain the same. Fuel is ignited in a cylinder, or chamber. Inside the sealed, hollow cylinder is a piston (a solid cylinder) that is free to move up and down and is attached at the bottom to a crankshaft. The energy created by the combustion, or burning, of the fuel pushes down on the piston. The movement of the piston turns the crankshaft, which then transfers that movement through various gears to the desired destination, such as the drive wheels in an automobile.

Basic principles

The most common internal-combustion engines are the piston-type gasoline engines used in most automobiles. In an engine, the cylinder is housed inside an engine block strong enough to contain the explosions of fuel. Inside the cylinder is a piston that fits the cylinder precisely. Pistons generally are dome-shaped on top, and hollow at the bottom. In a four-stroke engine, the piston completes one up-and-down cycle in four strokes: intake, compression, power, and exhaust.

The first stroke, the intake stroke, begins when the piston is at the top of the cylinder, called the cylinder head. As it is drawn down, it creates a vacuum in the cylinder. This is because the piston and the cylinder form an airtight space. This vacuum helps to draw the fuel-air mixture into the cylinder through an open intake valve, which closes when the piston reaches the bottom of the cylinder.

On the next stroke, called the compression stroke, the piston is pushed up inside the cylinder, compressing or squeezing the fuel-air mixture into a tighter and tighter space. The compression of the mixture against the top of the cylinder causes the air to heat up, which in turn heats the mixture. Compressing the fuel-air mixture also makes it easier to ignite and makes the resulting explosion more powerful. There is less space for the expanding gases of the explosion to flow, which means they will push harder against the piston in order to escape.

At the top of the compression stroke, the fuel-air mixture is ignited by a spark from a spark plug placed in the cylinder head, causing an explosion that pushes the piston down. This stroke is called the power stroke, and this is the stroke that turns the crankshaft.

The final stroke, the exhaust stroke, takes the piston upward again, expelling the exhaust gases created by the explosion from the cylinder through an exhaust valve. When the piston reaches the top of the cylinder, it begins the four-step process again.

Development of the internal-combustion engine

In 1824, French physicist Nicholas Carnot (1796–1832) published a book that set out the principles of an internal-combustion engine that would use an inflammable mixture of gas vapor and air. Basing his work

The major components of an internal-combustion engine. (Reproduced by permission of The Gale Group.)

INTERNAL COMBUSTION ENGINE

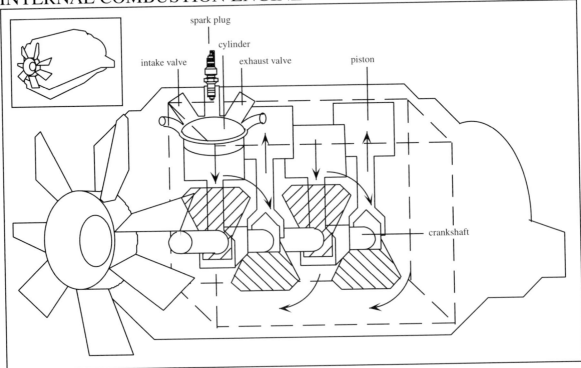

spark plug

cylinder

intake valve   exhaust valve   piston

crankshaft

on Carnot's principles, another Frenchman named Jean-Joseph-Étienne Lenoir (1822–1900) presented the world with its first workable internal-combustion engine in 1859. Lenoir's motor was a two-cycle (two-stroke), one-cylinder engine with slide valves that used coal gas as a fuel. A battery supplied the electrical charge to ignite the gas after it was drawn into the cylinder. In 1862, another Frenchman, Alphonse-Eugène Beau de Rochas (1815–1893), designed a four-stroke engine that would overcome many problems associated with the gas engines of that time.

Two-stroke engines eliminate the intake and exhaust strokes, combining them with the compression and power strokes. This allows for a lighter, more powerful engine—relative to the engine's size—requiring a less complex design. But the two-stroke cycle is a less efficient method of burning fuel. A residue of unburned fuel remains inside the cylinder, which hinders combustion. The two-stroke engine also ignites its fuel twice as often as a four-stroke engine, which increases the wear on the engine's parts. Two-stroke engines are therefore used mostly where a smaller engine is required, such as on some motorcycles and with small tools.

An internal-combustion engine can have anywhere from one to twelve or more cylinders, all acting together in a precisely timed sequence to drive the crankshaft. Automobiles generally have four-, six-, or eight-cylinder engines, although two-cylinder and twelve-cylinder engines are also available. The number of cylinders affects the engine's displacement, that is, the total volume of fuel passed through the cylinders. A larger displacement allows more fuel to be burned, creating more energy to drive the crankshaft.

In the case of an engine with two or more cylinders, however, the spark from the spark plugs must be directed to each cylinder in turn. The sequence of firing the cylinders must be timed so that while one piston is in its power stroke, another piston is in its compression stroke. In this way, the force exerted on the crankshaft can be kept constant, allowing the engine to run smoothly. The number of cylinders affects the smoothness of the engine's operation: the more cylinders, the more constant the force on the crankshaft and the more smoothly the engine will run.

In addition to piston-driven, gas-powered internal-combustion engines, other internal-combustion engines have been developed, such as the Wankel engine and the gas turbine engine. Jet engines and diesel engines are also powered by internal combustion.

[See also **Diesel engine; Jet engine**]

International Ultraviolet Explorer

Developed during the 1970s, the International Ultraviolet Explorer (IUE) was a joint project between the National Aeronautics and Space Administration (NASA); Particle Physics and Astronomy Research Council (PPARC), formerly known as the Science and Engineering Research Council of the United Kingdom (SERC); and the European Space Agency (ESA). The IUE was built to explore astronomical objects such as stars, comets, galaxies, and supernovae that exist in the ultraviolet portion of space. The IUE was defined as an "explorer class" mission. These missions are smaller in scope and the objective is a particular task, such as the study of ultraviolet radiation. Ultraviolet radiation is electromagnetic radiation (radiation that transmits energy through the interaction of electricity and magnetism) of a wavelength just shorter than the violet (shortest wavelength) end of the visible light spectrum.

IUE explores ultraviolet radiation

The Earth's ozone layer blocks ultraviolet radiation—which is harmful to humans—from penetrating the atmosphere. But the blockage makes it difficult to study ultraviolet radiation from the Earth's surface. In order to better understand ultraviolet radiation, an observatory must be created and sent beyond the Earth's atmosphere where the ozone layer does not interfere with the ultraviolet radiation. The IUE was such an observatory; it observed astronomical objects from space and relayed the information back to scientists on Earth.

The IUE was launched in January 1978 aboard a Delta rocket and put into a geosynchronous orbit (an orbit that is fixed with respect to Earth). Weighing 1,420 pounds (645 kilograms), the IUE measured 14 feet by 5 feet by 5 feet (4.3 meters by 1.5 meters by 1.5 meters) and was powered by 2 solar panels. The IUE was equipped with a 17.7-inch (45-centimeter) telescope hooked up with two spectrographs (instruments that photograph spectra) that could record ultraviolet wavelengths and transmit the information back to observatories on Earth. At the time, the IUE was the only satellite observatory that worked continually 24 hours a day.

While the IUE was orbiting Earth, astronomers monitored the information that the IUE was transmitting. Scientists at the Goddard Space Flight Center (GSFC) in Greenbelt, Maryland, handled IUE operations for sixteen hours a day and scientists at the Villafranca Satellite Tracking Station (VILSPA) in Spain operated the IUE for the other eight hours

Words to Know

Geosynchronous orbit: When placed in orbit at an altitude of 22,241 miles (35,786 kilometers) above the surface of Earth, a satellite completes one orbit around Earth at the same time Earth completes one revolution on its axis. This means the satellite remains stationary over a specific location on Earth and is said to be synchronized with Earth.

Ozone layer: The atmospheric layer of approximately 15 to 30 miles (24 to 48 kilometers) above Earth's surface in which the concentration of ozone is significantly higher than in other parts of the atmosphere and that protects the lower atmosphere from harmful solar radiation.

Spectrum: Range of individual wavelengths of radiation produced when white light is broken down into its component colors when it passes through a prism or is broken apart by some other means. (Plural: spectra.)

Ultraviolet radiation: Electromagnetic radiation (energy) of a wavelength just shorter than the violet (shortest wavelength) end of the visible light spectrum and thus with higher energy than visible light.

of the day. The ultraviolet telescope mounted on the IUE continually gathered information on astronomical objects.

By studying the light that is either emitted (thrown off) or absorbed by a celestial body (an object in the sky, such as a star, the Moon, or the Sun), scientists can learn about the activities that occur in space. They do this through the field of ultraviolet astronomy, the study of the dark absorption lines or bright emission lines of a spectrum. A spectrum comprises the colors of red, orange, yellow, green, blue, indigo, and violet. These colors travel at different wavelengths, decreasing in length from red (the longest) to violet (the shortest). When sunlight enters the atmosphere, materials present there break up sunlight into its component colors through reflection (bouncing off an object), refraction (bending through an object), or diffraction (bending around the edge of an object). It is from the individual spectrum lines that astronomers can understand the makeup of stars, galaxies, and other astronomical objects. For example, the more energy a star emits, the brighter it appears and the more ultraviolet wavelengths it sends off. The IUE allowed astronomers to better understand why the atmospheres of some stars are so hot and burn so brightly.

IUE highlights

The IUE made history when it helped make the first identification of an exploding star, named Supernova 1978A. In March 1996, the IUE observed the nucleus of the Comet Hyakutake as it underwent chemical changes during its five-day breakup. As the ultraviolet telescope continually sent back pictures to Earth, scientists learned that every time the comet passed the Sun, it ejected ten tons of water every second and that the eventual breakup of the comet involved only a very small piece of the comet. Other major milestones that the IUE aided in the study of are stellar winds (charged particles ejected from a star's surface); hot gas around the Milky Way (a galaxy that includes a few hundred billion stars, the Sun, and our solar system); the size of active galaxies; and stars with magnetic fields and surface activity.

Originally built to last five years, the IUE lasted almost nineteen years. During its lengthy service to the astronomy community, it did suffer some minor mechanical problems. Although engineers were

Technicians looking over the International Ultraviolet Explorer during magnetic checks, at Goddard Space Flight Center. *(Reproduced by permission of The Corbis Corporation.)*

able to keep the IUE functioning at various capacity levels, the final shut-down occurred on September 30, 1996, after a joint decision by NASA and ESA.

The IUE was awarded the U.S. Presidential Award for Design Excellence. It is considered one of the great success stories of astronomy as it made observations of over 100,000 astronomical objects during its use. Scientists from all over the world have enjoyed the information the IUE was able to collect. Over 3,500 scientific articles have been generated from this information, which is the most productive for any observatory satellite to date. Because of its endurance of almost nineteen years, the IUE was able to help astronomers gain a better understanding of ultraviolet astronomy.

On June 7, 1992, NASA launched the successor to the IUE, another Explorer-class mission, called the Extreme Ultraviolet Explorer (EUVE). This satellite went beyond the coverage of the IUE due its more powerful telescope.

[*See also* **Ultraviolet astronomy**]

Internet

The Internet is a vast network that connects many independent networks and links computers at different locations. It enables computer users throughout the world to communicate and to share information in a variety of ways. Its evolution into the World Wide Web made it easy to use for those with no prior computer training.

History

The Internet could not exist until the modern computer came to be. The first electronic computers were developed during the 1940s, and these early machines were so large—mainly because of all the bulky vacuum tubes they needed to perform calculations—that they often took up an entire room by themselves. They were also very expensive, and only a few corporations and government agencies could afford to own one. The decade of the 1950s proved to be one of silent conflict and tension between the Soviet Union and the United States—a period called the "cold war"—and computers naturally came to play a large role in those nations' military planning. Since each country was obsessed with the possibility of a deliberate or accidental nuclear war breaking out, the United States

Words to Know

HTML: HyperText Markup Language, used in writing pages for the World Wide Web; it lets the text include codes that define font, layout, embedded graphics, and hypertext links.

HTTP: HyperText Transfer Protocol, which is the way World Wide Web pages are transferred over the Internet.

Hypertext: System of writing and displaying text that enables the text to be linked in multiple ways, to be available on several levels of detail, and to contain links to related documents.

Links: Electronic connections between pieces of information.

Network: A system made up of lines or paths for data flow that includes nodes where the lines intersect and where the data can flow into different lines.

Packets: Small batches of data that computers exchange.

Protocols: Rules or standards for operations and behavior.

World Wide Web: A hypermedia system that is a graphical map for the Internet, that is simple to understand, and that helps users navigate around Internet sites.

began to consider how it might protect its valuable lines of communication in case such a disaster did occur. By the 1960s, both nations had become increasingly dependent on their rapidly-improving computing technologies, and the United States eventually developed a means of linking its major defense-related computer facilities together (to form a network). In 1969, the U.S. Department of Defense began a network of university and military computers that it called ARPANET (Advanced Research Projects Agency Network).

Packet switching

The major characteristic of ARPANET was the way it used the new idea called "packet switching." What this does is break up data—or information to be transmitted from one computer to another—into pieces or "packets" of equal-size message units. These pieces or packets are then sent separately to their destination where they are finally reassembled to reform the complete message. So by "packet switching" data, a message is sent in pieces or segments, each of which may travel a different route to the same destination, where it is eventually put back together, no matter how or which way it got there. For defense purposes, this system seemed ideal since if there were any working path to the final destination, no matter how indirect, the new network would find it and use it to get the message through. In 1970, ARPANET began operations between only four universities, but by the end of 1971, ARPANET was linking twenty-three host computers.

How computers could talk to one another

As this system slowly grew, it became apparent that eventually the computers at each different location would need to follow the same rules and procedures if they were to communicate with one another. In fact, if they all went their separate ways and spoke a different "language" and operated under different instructions, then they could never really be linked together in any meaningful way. More and more, the scientists, engineers, librarians, and computer experts who were then using ARPANET found that the network was both highly complex and very difficult to use. As early as 1972, users were beginning to form a sort of bulletin board for what we now call e-mail (electronic mail). This made the need for common procedures even more obvious, and in 1974, what came to be called a common protocol (pronounced PRO-tuh-call) was finally developed. Protocols are sets of rules that standardize how something is done so that everyone knows what to do and what to expect—sort of like the rules of a game. This common language was known as a Transmission Control Protocol/Internet Protocol (TCP/IP).

Open architecture

The development of this protocol proved to be a crucial step in the development of a real, working network since it established certain rules or procedures that eventually would allow the network really to expand. One of the keys of the protocol was that it was designed with what was called "open architecture." This meant that each network would be able to work on its own and not have to modify itself in any way in order to be part of the network. This would be taken care of by a "gateway" (usually a larger computer) that each network would have whose special software linked it to the outside world. In order to make sure that data was transmitted quickly, the gateway software was designed so that it would not hold on to any of the data that passed through it. This not only sped things up, but it also removed any possibility of censorship or central control. Finally, data would always follow the fastest available route, and all networks were allowed to participate.

Computer address

In practice, the new TCP/IP set up a system that is often compared to a postal system. The information being sent or the "data packets" would have headers just as a letter has an address on its envelope. The header would therefore specify where it came from and what its destination was. Just as everyone's postal rules (protocols) state that all mail must be in an envelope or some sort of package and that it must have postage and a destination address, so TCP/IP said that every computer connected to the network must have a unique address. When the electronic packet was sent to the routing computer, it would sort through tables of addresses just as a mail sorter in a post office sorts through zip codes. It would then select the best connection or available route and send it along. On the receiving end, the TCP/IP software made sure all the pieces of the packet were there and then it put them back together in proper order, ready to be used. It makes no difference (other than speed) to the network how the data was transmitted, and one computer can communicate with another using regular phone lines, fiber-optic cables, radio links, or even satellites.

Personal computers and domain names

All of this took some time, but by the beginning of 1983, when the TCP/IP was ready to go and finally adopted, the Internet—or a network of networks—was finally born. To this point, most of the business on the "Net," as it came to be called, was science-oriented. About this same time, however, the microcomputer revolution was also starting to be felt. Called "personal computers," these new, smaller, desktop-size computers began slowly to enter businesses and homes, eventually transforming the notion of what a computer was. Until this time, a computer was a very large, super-expensive, anonymous-looking machine (called a "mainframe") that only corporations could afford. Now however, a computer was a friendly, nearly-portable, *personal* machine that had a monitor or screen like a television set. As more and more individuals purchased a personal computer and eventually learned about a way of talking to another computer (via e-mail), the brand-new Internet soon began to experience the problems of its own success.

By 1984, it was apparent that something had to be done to straighten out and simplify the naming system for each "host" computer (the host was the "server" computer that was actually linked to the Internet). That year, the system called "Domain Name Servers" was created. This new system organized Internet addresses into various "domains" or categories—such as governmental (.gov), commercial (.com), educational (.edu), military (.mil), network sites (.net), or international organizations (.org)—that were tacked onto the end of the address. Host or server names now were not only much easier to remember, but the alphabetical addresses themselves actually stood for a longer coded sequence of numbers that the computer needed in order to specifically identify an address. Thus, a person needed only to use a fairly short alphabetical address, which itself contained the more complex numerical sequence. By 2001, however, an entire batch of additional domain names (.biz, .info, .name, .museum, .aero, .coop, and .pro) had to be created to account for the increase in both specialization and use. This domain expansion is similar to the phone company issuing new area codes.

NSFNET

By the mid-1980s, a second, larger network had grown up in the United States, and it would eventually absorb ARPANET. The National Science Foundation established its own cross-country network, called NSFNET, in order to encourage increased network communication by col-

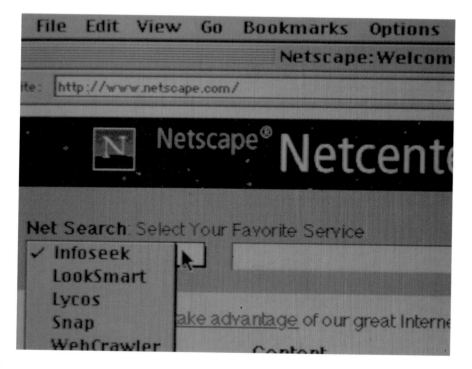

The Internet is searchable by many means, such as the many search engines. *(Reproduced by permission of Field Mark Publications.)*

leges and universities. NSFNET adopted the TCP/IP rules, but it did not allow its system to be used for non-educational purposes. This policy proved to be very important since it eventually led businesses to create networks of their own, and also encouraged several private "providers" to open for business. In 1987, the first subscription-based commercial Internet company, called UUNET, was founded. As the end of the 1980s approached, the Internet was growing, but it was still not the place for a beginner. The main problem was that every time users wanted to do something different on it (such as e-mail or file transfer), they had to know how to operate an entirely separate program. Commands had to be either memorized or reference manuals had to be constantly consulted. The Internet was not "user-friendly."

World Wide Web

The development of what came to be called the World Wide Web in 1991 marked the real breakthrough of the Internet to a mass audience of users. The World Wide Web is really a software package that was based on "hypertext." In hypertext, links are "embedded" in the text (meaning that certain key words are either underlined or appear in a contrasting sdifferent color) that the user can then click on with a mouse to be taken to another site containing more information. It was the development of the Web that made usage of the Internet really take off, since it was simple to understand and use and enabled even new users to be able to explore or "surf" the Net. Without the World Wide Web, the Internet probably would have remained a mystery to those huge numbers of people who either had no computer expertise or wanted any computer training.

The Web developed a new set of rules called HTTP (HyperText Transfer Protocol) that simplified address writing and that used a new programming language called HTML (HyperText Markup Language). This special language allowed users easily to jump (by clicking on a link) from one document or information resource to another. In 1993, the addition of the program called Mosaic proved to be the final breakthrough in terms of ease-of-use. Before Mosaic, the Web

Many safeties have been set up for home usage of the Internet to insure that younger surfers aren't seeing inappropriate content. *(Reproduced by permission of Archive Photos, Inc.)*

was limited only to text or words. However, as a "graphical browser," the Mosaic program included multimedia links, meaning that a user could click on icons (pictures of symbols) and view pictures, listen to audio, and even see video. By 1995, with the addition of sound and graphics and the emergence of such large commercial providers as America Online (AOL), Prodigy, and Compuserv, interest and usage of the Internet really took off.

By the beginning of the twenty-first century, the Internet had become a vast network involving millions of users connected by many independent networks spanning over 170 countries throughout the world. People use it to communicate (probably the most popular use), and hundreds of millions of e-mail messages electronically fly across the globe every day. People also use it as they would a library, to do research of all types on all sorts of subjects. On almost any major subject, a user can find text, photos, video, and be referred to other books and sources. The

Internet

The Internet is an invaluable research tool in schools, libraries, and homes around the world. *(Reproduced by permission of Field Mark Publications.)*

Internet also has commercial possibilities, and users can find almost any type of product being sold there. A person with a credit card can book an airline flight, rent a beach home and car, reserve tickets to a performance, and buy nearly anything else he or she desires. Some businesses benefit from this more than others, but there is no dismissing the fact that the Internet has changed the way business is conducted.

Used daily for thousands of other reasons, the Internet is many things to many people. It is a world-wide broadcasting medium, a mechanism for interacting with others, and a mechanism for obtaining and disseminating information. Today, the Internet has become an integral part of our world, and most would agree that its usefulness is limited only by our imagination.

[*See also* **Computer software**]

Interstellar matter

The interstellar medium—the space between the stars—consists of nearly empty space. It is the vacuum of the universe. It would be totally empty if not for a smattering of gas atoms and tiny solid particles—interstellar matter.

On average, the interstellar matter in our region of the galaxy consists of about one atom of gas per cubic centimeter and 25 to 50 microscopic solid particles per cubic kilometer. In contrast, the air at sea level on Earth contains about 1,019 molecules of gas per cubic centimeter.

In some regions of space, however, the concentration of interstellar matter is thousands of times greater than average. Where there is a large enough concentration of gas and particles (also called cosmic dust), clouds form. Most of the time these clouds are so thin they are invisible. At other times they are dense enough to be seen and are called nebulae (plural for nebula).

Cosmic dust

Cosmic dust accounts for only 1 percent of the total mass in the interstellar medium; the other 99 percent is gas. Scientists believe the dust is primarily composed of carbon and silicate material (silicon, oxygen, and metallic ions), possibly with solid carbon dioxide and frozen water and ammonia. A dark nebula is a relatively dense cloud of cosmic dust. The nebula is dark because much of the starlight in its path is either absorbed or reflected by dust particles. When starlight is reflected, it shines off in every direction, meaning only a small percentage is sent in the direction of Earth. This process effectively blocks most of the starlight from Earth's view.

Even individual particles of cosmic dust affect the quality of starlight. Random dust particles absorb or reflect some light from various stars, causing them to appear far dimmer than they actually are. Scientists have theorized that without the presence of cosmic dust, the Milky Way would shine so brightly that it would be light enough on Earth to read at night.

Most dark nebulae resemble slightly shimmering, dark curtains. However, in cases where a dense cloud of dust is situated near a particularly bright star, the scattering of light may be more pronounced, forming a reflection nebula. This is a region where the dust itself is illuminated by the reflected light.

Interstellar gas

In contrast to solid particles, interstellar gas is transparent. Hydrogen accounts for about three-quarters of the gas. The remainder is helium plus trace amounts of nitrogen, oxygen, carbon, sulfur, and possibly other elements.

While interstellar gas is generally cold, the gas near very hot stars is heated and ionized (electrically charged) by ultraviolet radiation given off by those stars. The glowing areas of ionized gas are called emission nebulae. Two well-known examples of emission nebulae are the Orion nebula, visible through binoculars just south of the hunter's belt in the constellation of the same name, and the Lagoon nebula in the constellation Sagittarius. The Orion nebula is punctuated by dark patches of cosmic dust.

Interstellar space also contains over 60 types of polyatomic (containing more than one atom) molecules. The most common substance is molecular hydrogen (H_2); others include water, carbon monoxide, and ammonia. Since these molecules are broken down by starlight, they are found primarily in dense, dark nebulae where they are protected from the light by cosmic dust. These nebulae—known as molecular clouds—are enormous. They stretch across several light-years and are 1,000 to 1,000,000 times as massive as the Sun.

An artist's impression of the birth of two stars from clouds of interstellar matter. As the stars begin to form, their increasing gravity pulls more of the surrounding gases, which will be incorporated into the stars and used as fuel during their lifetime. *(Reproduced by permission of Photo Researchers, Inc.)*

Origin of interstellar matter

Scientists have proposed various theories as to the origins of interstellar matter. Some matter has been ejected into space by stars, particularly from stars in the final stages of their lives. As a star depletes the supply of fuel on its surface, the chemical composition of the surrounding interstellar medium is altered. Massive red giant stars have been observed ejecting matter, probably composed of heavy elements such as aluminum, calcium, and titanium. This material may then condense into solid particles, which combine with hydrogen, oxygen, carbon, and nitrogen when they enter interstellar clouds.

It is also possible that interstellar matter represents material that did not condense into stars when the galaxy formed billions of years ago. Evidence supporting this theory can be found in the fact that new stars are born within clouds of interstellar gas and dust.

[*See also* **Galaxy; Star**]

Invertebrates

Invertebrates are animals without backbones. This simple definition hides the tremendous diversity found within this group which includes protozoa (single-celled animals), corals, sponges, sea urchins, starfish, sand dollars, worms, snails, clams, spiders, crabs, and insects. In fact, more than 98 percent of the nearly two million described species are invertebrates. They range in size from less than one millimeter to several meters long. Invertebrates display a fascinating diversity of body forms, means of locomotion, and feeding habits.

Invertebrates are ectotherms (cold-blooded): they warm their bodies by absorbing heat from their surroundings. Most invertebrates live in water or spend at least some part of their life in water. The external layers of aquatic invertebrates are generally thin and permeable to water. This structure allows the ready exchange of gases needed to keep the animal alive. Some aquatic vertebrates do have specialized respiratory (breathing) structures on their body surface. Aquatic invertebrates feed by ingesting their prey directly, by filter feeding, or by actively capturing prey.

Some groups of invertebrates live on land. Common examples include the earthworms, insects, and spiders. These invertebrates need to have special structures to deal with life on land. For example, earthworms have strong muscles for crawling and burrowing and, since drying out on land is a problem for them, they secrete mucous to keep their bodies moist. Insects and spiders move by means of several pairs of legs and are waterproof.

[*See also* **Arachnids; Arthropods; Butterflies; Cockroaches; Corals; Crustaceans; Insects; Mollusks; Protozoa**]

Ninety-eight percent of animals are invertebrates. *(Reproduced by permission of The Gale Group.)*

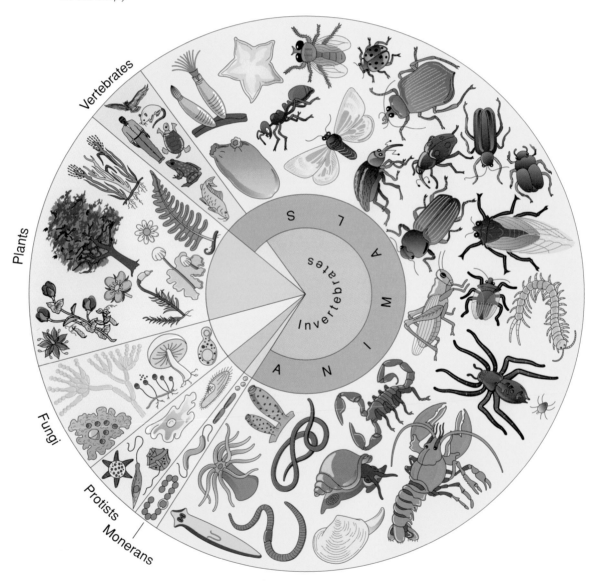

Ionization

Ionization is the process in which one or more electrons are removed from an atom or molecule. The charged particle that results is called an ion. As an example, consider an atom of oxygen. An oxygen atom consists of a nucleus containing eight protons and eight neutrons. Each proton carries a single positive electrical charge, and each neutron is electrically neutral. The oxygen atom also contains eight electrons, each carrying a single negative electrical charge. With eight positive charges and eight negative charges, an oxygen atom is neutral.

Some of the electrons in an atom can be removed rather easily. If an oxygen atom should lose one electron, for example, it would then have eight positive charges and only seven negative charges. Overall the atom would have an electric charge of +1. If two electrons were to be removed, it would have a charge of +2.

Under some circumstances, the oxygen atom could also gain electrons. If it gained one electron, it would then have eight positive charges and nine negative charges, or an overall charge of −1. The charged atoms of oxygen in all of the above cases are no longer called atoms. They are called ions. If they carry a positive charge, they are known as cations, and if they carry a negative charge they are known as anions.

Molecules can also be ionized. Molecules are collections of atoms held together by shared pairs of electrons. If an electron in a molecule is removed, the portion of the molecule that remains becomes charged, just as is the case with atoms. For example, if a molecule of nitrogen loses an electron, it becomes a cation with a charge of +1.

Ionization energy

Electrons in an atom are attracted to the atomic nucleus by electrical forces. An electron is negatively charged; the nucleus is positively charged. Since opposite charges attract each other, an electron tends to stay with its atomic nucleus.

In order to remove an electron from an atom, then, energy must be provided to overcome the force of attraction of the nucleus. That energy is called ionization energy.

The energy needed to remove an electron differs from atom to atom. Consider the difference between hydrogen and sodium. Hydrogen has only one electron, located fairly close to its nucleus. A good deal of energy is needed to overcome the attraction of the hydrogen nucleus for its

▼ Words to Know

Crystal: A solid composed of positively and negatively charged ions.

Dissociation: The process by which ions are set free from a crystal, usually in water solution.

Ion: A molecule or atom that has lost one or more electrons and is, therefore, electrically charged.

Ionization energy: The amount of energy required to completely remove an electron from an atom or molecule, thereby creating a positively charged ion.

Molecule: The smallest particle of which a compound consists, made of two or more atoms bonded to each other by shared pairs of electrons.

electron. Sodium has 11 electrons, one of which is at a relatively great distance from the nucleus. The force of attraction by the nucleus for that outermost electron is small, compared to the force in a hydrogen atom. The outermost sodium electron can be removed with a relatively small amount of energy.

This comparison can be confirmed by looking at the first ionization energy for both hydrogen and sodium. The first ionization energy is the amount of energy required to remove the first electron from an atom. For hydrogen, that number is 1,312 kilojoules per mole, and for sodium it is 495.9 kilojoules per mole. (A mole is a unit used to represent a certain number of particles, usually atoms or molecules.)

Similar measurements can be made for removing the second electron, third electron, fourth electron, and so on, from an atom. These measurements are known as the second ionization energy, third ionization energy, fourth ionization energy, and so on.

Ionization in solution. The term ionization also has a second meaning when used in discussions of solutions. The way substances behave electrically in water solution is often very different from the way they behave as solids or gases. As an example, consider the compound known as acetic acid. Acetic acid is a liquid that does not conduct an electric current. Yet, when acetic acid is added to water, the solution that is formed *does* conduct an electric current.

In order for a solution to conduct an electric current, ions must be present. Pure acetic acid is made of molecules. It contains no ions. If you pass an electric current into acetic acid, nothing will happen because no ions are present. An important change takes place, however, when acetic acid is added to water. Water molecules have the ability to tear acetic acid molecules apart, breaking them down into hydrogen ions and acetate ions. Now that ions are present, the water solution of acetic acid can conduct an electric current. This process is known as ionization because ions are produced from a substance (acetic acid) that did not contain them originally.

Dissociation. A similar story about the conductivity and nonconductivity of sodium chloride could be told. If the two ends of a battery are attached to a large crystal of sodium chloride, no electric current will flow. One might guess that this result indicates that no ions are present in sodium chloride. However, that is not the case.

Indeed, a crystal of sodium chloride is made up entirely of ions, positively charged sodium ions and negatively charged chloride ions. The problem is, however, that these ions are held together very tightly by electrical forces. Sodium ions are bound tightly to chloride ions, and vice versa.

The situation changes, however, when sodium chloride is added to water. Water molecules are able to tear apart sodium ions and chloride ions in much the same way they tear apart acetic acid molecules. Once the sodium ions and chloride ions are no longer bound tightly to each other, they are free to roam through the salt/water solution.

The name given to this change is dissociation. The term means that ions already existed in the sodium chloride crystal before it was put into water. Water did not create the ions, it only set them free. It is this difference between creating ions and setting them free that distinguishes ionization from dissociation.

Island

An island is a relatively small area of land that is completely surrounded by water. It is impossible to give a total number to the islands that exist on the surface of the planet. As a result of erosion or rising sea level, some islands drown over time. The longest surviving islands usually last no more than 5 to 10 million years (Earth is 4.5 billion years old). Ongoing volcanic activity continues to create new islands and to add to existing ones. On November 14, 1963, a underwater volcanic explosion off

Words to Know

Barrier islands: Long, thin, sandy stretches of land that lie in shallow waters parallel to a mainland coast.

Continental shelves: Submerged, gradually sloping ledges of continents.

Hot spot: Plumes of magma welling up from Earth's crust.

Island arc: Curved row of islands of volcanic origin that develops where two plates converge, usually near the edge of a continent.

Magma: Hot, liquid material that underlies areas of volcanic activity; magma at Earth's surface is called lava.

Plate tectonics: Geological theory stating that Earth's crust is divided into a series of vast platelike sections that move as distinct masses over the planet's surface.

the southern coast of Iceland created the island of Surtsey, which continues to gain land as the ongoing lava flows cool.

The eight largest islands on Earth are (in descending order): Greenland, New Guinea, Borneo, Madagascar, Baffin Island, Sumatra, Honshu (largest of the Japanese islands), and Great Britain. Islands can be divided into two types: continental or oceanic.

Continental islands

Continental islands are parts of the continental shelves—the submerged, gradually sloping ledges of continents. These islands are formed in one of two ways: rising ocean waters either cover coastal areas, leaving only the summits of coastal highlands above water, or cut off a peninsula or similar piece of land jutting out from the mainland. Continental islands lie in shallow water, usually less than 600 feet (180 meters) deep. Greenland and Newfoundland (off the eastern coast of Canada) are examples of continental islands. A drop in sea level would be sufficient to connect these islands to the North American continent.

Long, thin, sandy stretches of land that lie in shallow waters parallel to a mainland coast are called barrier islands. These are technically not continental islands since they are formed by the erosion of mainland rock (sand). The sand is carried to coastal areas by rivers and then carried offshore by strong waves and other ocean currents.

Oceanic islands

Oceanic islands are not scattered haphazardly about the deep ocean waters. They arise from volcanic activity on the ocean floor. Over time, the cooled lava forms mountains, the tops of which rise above the surface of the ocean as islands. According to the geological theory of plate

An island off the east coast of the Malay peninsula. *(Reproduced by permission of The Stock Market.)*

tectonics, Earth's crust is divided into a series of vast platelike sections that move as distinct masses over the planet's surface. Most oceanic islands are formed as oceanic plates move over fixed hot spots (plumes of magma or lava welling up from the crust). Some oceanic islands are situated above the boundaries where oceanic plates converge or come together, while others arise where plates diverge or spread apart (a process called seafloor spreading).

The Hawaiian-Emperor island chain in the north Pacific Ocean formed as a result of a plate moving over a thermal plume of magma from a fixed hot spot. The hot spot is believed to be causing the currently active volcanoes of Mauna Loa and Kilauea on the island of Hawaii.

When two plates converge, the plate carrying the heavier crust dips under, or subducts, the plate carrying the lighter crust. At the point of subduction, a deep trench develops. Parallel to it, on the lighter plate, volcanic action produces a row of islands. These island groups are called island arcs, after their curved pattern. The Aleutian Islands, off the southwest coast of Alaska, are such islands.

Island ecosystems

Islands often contain a strange mix of plants and animals. Because oceanic islands are isolated by their surrounding waters, they are home to only a few species of animals. Many of these animal species are found nowhere else on the planet. The small size of islands also prevents them from supporting a larger number of animal species. A few seabirds and insects exist in greater numbers since they are able to migrate over the waters separating islands. Plant life on islands is most abundant, as seeds are carried by winds, water currents, and birds from remote lands.

Island ecosystems (communities of plants, animals, and microorganisms) are delicate and balanced. Over time, they have reached a steady state—what is taken out of the environment is replaced. The relationship between predators and prey remain constant: those that die are replaced by newborns. The introduction of other life-forms into the closed system of an island, therefore, can have dramatic immediate effects. Changes brought about by humans is particularly devastating to islands. For example, domestic goats and rabbits introduced by human colonizers can completely rob a small island of succulent vegetation in less than a year. Dogs can turn every small mammal into prey.

Such changes to an island's ecosystem can result in the extinction of animal or plant species, many of which are not even known. Scientists are increasingly concerned about raising awareness of the special features of islands and their contributions to geological and evolutionary knowledge.

[*See also* **Coast and beach; Plate tectonics; Volcano**]

Isotope

Isotopes are two forms of an element with the same atomic number but different mass number. The existence of isotopes can be understood by reviewing the structure of atoms.

All atoms contain three kinds of basic particles: protons, neutrons, and electrons. (Hydrogen is the only exception to this statement; most hydrogen atoms contain no neutrons.) The protons and neutrons in an atom are found in the atomic nucleus, while the electrons are found in the space around the nucleus.

The number of protons in a nucleus defines an atom. Hydrogen atoms all have one proton in their nucleus; helium atoms all have two protons in their nucleus; lithium atoms all have three protons in their nucleus; and so on. The number of protons in an atom's nucleus is called its atomic number. Hydrogen has an atomic number of 1; helium, an atomic number of 2; and lithium, an atomic number of 3.

But atoms of the same element can have different numbers of neutrons. Some helium nuclei, for example, have two neutrons; others have only one. The mass number of an atom is the total number of protons and neutrons in the atom's nucleus. The two-neutron atom of helium has a mass number of four (two protons plus two neutrons). The one-neutron atom of helium has a mass number of three (two protons plus one neutron).

Another way of defining isotopes, then, is to say that they are different forms of an atom with the same number of protons but different numbers of neutrons.

Most elements have at least two stable isotopes. The term stable here means not radioactive. Twenty elements, including fluorine, sodium, aluminum, phosphorus, and gold, have only one stable isotope. By contrast, tin has the largest number of stable isotopes of any element, ten.

Representing isotopes

Isotopes are commonly represented in one of two ways. First, they may be designated by writing the name of the element followed by the mass number of the isotope. The two forms of helium are called helium-4 and helium-3. Second, isotopes may be designated by the chemical symbol of the element with a superscript that shows their mass number. The designations for the two isotopes of helium are ^{4}He and ^{3}He.

Radioactive isotopes

A radioactive isotope is an isotope that spontaneously breaks apart, changing into some other isotope. As an example, potassium has a radioactive isotope with mass number 40, ^{40}K or potassium-40. This isotope breaks down into a stable isotope of potassium, ^{39}K or potassium-39.

Radioactive isotopes are much more common than are stable isotopes. At least 1,000 radioactive isotopes occur in nature or have been produced synthetically in particle accelerators (atom-smashers) or nuclear reactors (devices used to control the release of energy from nuclear reactions).

Applications

Isotopes have many important applications in theoretical and practical research. The advantage of using two or more isotopes of the same element is that the isotopes will all have the same chemical properties but may differ from each other because of their mass differences. This difference allows scientists to separate one isotope from another. An important example of this process is the way isotopes were used to purify uranium during World War II (1939–45).

Two common isotopes of uranium exist, ^{235}U and ^{238}U. Of these two, ^{238}U is much more abundant, making up about 99.3 percent of the uranium found in nature. But only ^{235}U can be used in making nuclear weapons and nuclear reactors. Since both ^{235}U and ^{238}U have the same chemical properties, how can the valuable ^{235}U be separated from the more abundant, but valueless, ^{238}U?

One answer to this question was to convert natural uranium to a gas and then allow the gas to diffuse (spread out) through a porous barrier. Researchers found that the ^{235}U in the natural uranium was slightly less heavy than the ^{238}U, so it diffused through the barrier slightly more quickly. But because the difference in mass between the two isotopes is not very great, the diffusion had to be repeated many times before the two isotopes could be separated very well. Eventually, however, enough ^{235}U was collected by this process to make the world's first nuclear weapons.

[*See also* **Atomic mass; Carbon family; Dating techniques; Nuclear fission; Nuclear medicine; Periodic table; Radioactive tracers; Radioactivity; Spectrometry**]

J

Jet engine

A jet engine is a heat engine that is propelled in a forward direction as the result of the escape of hot gases from the rear of the engine. In an air-breathing jet engine, air entering the front of the engine is used to burn a fuel within the engine, producing the hot gases needed for propulsion (forward movement). Jet engines are used for the fastest commercial and military aircraft now available.

A cutaway of a turbojet engine. A jet engine works by sucking air into one end, compressing it, mixing it with fuel and burning it in the combustion chanber, and then expelling it with great force out the exhaust system. *(Reproduced by permission of The Gale Group.)*

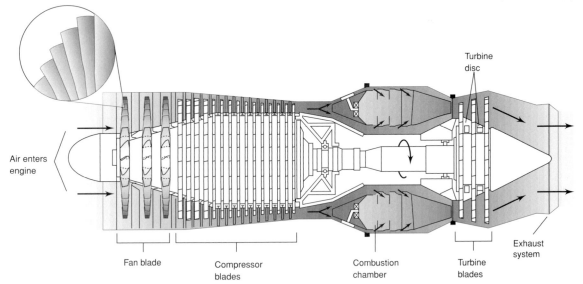

Air enters engine

Turbine disc

Exhaust system

Fan blade   Compressor blades   Combustion chamber   Turbine blades

Words to Know

Afterburner: A device added at the rear of a jet engine that adds additional fuel to the exhaust gases, increasing the efficiency of the engine's combustion.

Combustion: The process of burning; a chemical reaction, especially a rapid combination with oxygen, accompanied by heat and light.

Compress: To make more compact by using pressure.

Ramjet: A simple type of air-breathing jet engine in which incoming air is compressed and used to burn a jet fuel such as kerosene.

Turbojet: A type of air-breathing jet engine in which some of the exhaust gases produced in the engine are used to operate a compressor by which incoming air is reduced in volume and increased in pressure.

Turboprop: An engine in which an air-breathing jet engine is used to power a conventional propeller-driven aircraft.

Scientific principle behind jet engines

The scientific principle on which the jet engine operates was first stated in scientific terms by English physicist and mathematician Isaac Newton (1642–1727) in 1687. According to Newton's third law of motion, for every action there is an equal and opposite reaction. That principle can be illustrated by the behavior of a balloon filled with air. If the neck of the balloon is untied, gases begin to escape from the balloon. The escape of gases from the balloon is, in Newton's terms, an "action." The equal and opposite reaction resulting from the escape of gases is the movement of the balloon in a direction opposite to that of the movement of the gases. That is, as the air moves to the rear, the balloon moves forward.

Types of jet engines

Ramjets. The simplest of all jet engines is the ramjet. The ramjet consists of a long cylindrical metal tube open at both ends. The tube bulges in the middle and tapers off at both ends. As the engine moves forward at high speeds, the air entering it is automatically compressed (made more compact under pressure). The compressed air is then used to burn a fuel, usually a kerosene-like material. The hot gases produced during combustion within the engine are then expelled out the back of the engine. As the gases leave the back of the jet engine (the nozzle exit), they propel the engine—and the wing and airplane to which it is attached—in a forward direction.

A typical ramjet engine today has a length of about 13 feet (4 meters), a diameter of about 39 inches (1 meter), and a weight of about 1,000 pounds (450 kilograms). A ramjet engine of this design is capable of giving a maximum velocity of about Mach 4 (Mach 1 is equal to the speed of sound: 740 miles [1190 kilometers] per hour).

A jet aircraft with the engine cover open. (Reproduced by permission of Photo Researchers, Inc.)

Turbojets. A turbojet differs from a ramjet in that it contains a compressor attached to a turbine. The compressor consists of several rows of metal blades attached to a central shaft. The shaft, in turn, is attached to a turbine at the rear of the compressor. When air enters the inlet of a turbojet engine, some of it is directed to the core of the engine where the compressor is located. The compressor reduces the volume of the air and sends it into the combustion chamber under high pressure.

The exhaust gases formed in the combustion chamber have two functions. They exit the rear of the chamber, as in a ramjet, providing the engine with a forward thrust. At the same time, the gases pass over the blades of the turbine, causing it to spin on its axis. The spinning turbine operates the compressor at the front of the engine, making possible the continued compression of new incoming air. Unlike a ramjet engine, which only operates after a high speed has been attained, the turbojet engine operates continuously.

Turboprop engines. In a turboprop engine, a conventional propeller is attached to the turbine in a turbojet engine. As the turbine is turned by the series of reactions described above, it turns the airplane's propeller. Much greater propeller speeds can be attained by this combination than are possible with simple piston-driven propeller planes. However, propellers cannot operate at high air speeds. The maximum efficient speed at which turboprop airplanes can operate is less than 450 miles (724 kilometers) per hour.

Afterburners. No more than about one-quarter of all the oxygen entering the front of the jet engine is actually used to burn fuel within the engine. To make the process more efficient, some jet engines are also equipped with an afterburner. The afterburner is located directly behind the turbine in the jet engine. It consists of tubes out of which fuel is sprayed into the hot exhaust gases exiting the tubing. Combustion takes place in the afterburner, as it does in the combustion chamber, providing the engine with additional thrust.

Jupiter

Jupiter, the fifth planet from the Sun, is the largest and most massive planet in our solar system. It is 1,300 times larger than Earth, with more than 300 times the mass of Earth and 2.5 times the mass of all the other planets combined. It has a diameter over 88,000 miles (142,000 kilometers), more than eleven times Earth's diameter of 7,900 miles (12,700 kilometers). Lying about 480 million miles (770 million kilometers) from the Sun, Jupiter takes almost 12 years to complete one revolution.

With its 28 moons, Jupiter is considered a mini-solar system of its own. Before the twenty-first century, astronomers believed Jupiter had only 16 moons. But a rash of discoveries soon put the total at 28. The newly discovered satellites are highly different from Jupiter's more well-known moons. They are much smaller, with estimated diameters ranging from 1.8 to 5 miles (3 to 8 kilometers). Also, they have large and eccentric orbits. Some go around Jupiter in a clockwise direction, while others

Jupiter, as seen by *Voyager 1*. The planet is the most massive object in the solar system after the Sun; its mass is greater than that of all the other planets combined. *(Reproduced by permission of National Aeronautics and Space Administration.)*

orbit counter-clockwise. Astronomers speculate that Jupiter, while it was still young, captured the newly discovered moons from a group of small icy and rocky objects that orbit the Sun.

Jupiter is often the brightest object in the sky after the Sun and Venus. For some unknown reasons, it reflects light that is twice as intense as the sunlight that strikes it.

Jupiter has rings that are composed of small particles. Saturn, Uranus, and Neptune also have ring systems. It was only in late 1998 that

The four largest satellites of Jupiter are the Galilean satellites, named after seventeenth-century Italian astronomer Galileo Galilei. This composite image shows the four satellites to scale: Io (upper left), Europa (upper right), Ganymede (lower left), and Callisto (lower right). All but Europa are larger than our moon. Ganymede is larger than Mercury. *(Reproduced by permission of National Aeronautics and Space Administration.)*

Dr. Joseph Burns, astronomy professor at Cornell University, and a team of researchers figured out how Jupiter's rings are formed. After studying photos taken by the unmanned spacecraft *Galileo,* astronomers announced that Jupiter's rings are formed when cosmic debris (such as asteroids or particles of comets) are pulled and smashed into Jupiter's moons by the planet's powerful magnetic field. The resulting collision produces dust clouds that become the rings around the planet.

Through a telescope, Jupiter appears as a globe of colorful swirling bands. These bands may be a result of the planet's fast rotation. One day on Jupiter lasts only 10 hours (compared to a rotational period of 24 hours on Earth).

Jupiter's most outstanding feature is its Great Red Spot. The spot is actually a swirling, windy storm measuring 16,000 miles (25,700 kilometers) long and 8,700 miles (14,000 kilometers) wide, an area large enough to cover two Earths. The spot may get its red color from sulfur or phosphorus, but no one is sure. Beneath it lie three white oval areas. Each is a storm about the size of Mars.

The planet's origin

One theory about Jupiter's origin is that the planet is made of the original gas and dust that came together to form the Sun and planets. Since it so far from the Sun, its components may have undergone little or no change. A more recent theory, however, states that Jupiter was formed from ice and rock from comets, and that it grew by attracting other matter around it.

Astronomers have been observing Jupiter since the beginning of recorded time. In 1610, Italian astronomer Galileo Galilei (1564–1642) looked through his recently developed telescope and discovered the planet's four largest moons: Io, Europa, Ganymede, and Callisto.

Discoveries by the *Galileo* probe

In 1989, the 2.5-ton (2.3-metric ton) *Galileo* space probe was launched aboard the space shuttle *Atlantis.* On December 7, 1995, *Galileo* began orbiting Jupiter and dropped a mini-probe the size of an average backyard barbecue grill. The probe entered Jupiter's atmosphere at a speed of 106,000 miles (170,500 kilometers) per hour. Soon after, the probe released a parachute and floated down to the planet's hot surface. As it fell, intense winds blew it 300 miles (480 kilometers) horizontally. The probe spent 58 minutes taking extremely detailed pictures of Jupiter until its cameras stopped working at an altitude of about 100 miles (160 kilometers) below the top of the planet's cloud cover. Eight hours later, the probe was completely vaporized as temperatures reached 3,400°F (1,870°C).

What the probe discovered first was a belt of radiation 31,000 miles (49,900 kilometers) above Jupiter's clouds, containing the strongest radio waves in the solar system. It next encountered Jupiter's swirling clouds and found that they contain water, helium, hydrogen, carbon, sulfur, and neon, but in much smaller quantities than expected. It also found gaseous krypton and xenon, but in greater amounts than previously estimated.

Scientists had predicted the probe would encounter three or four dense cloud layers of ammonia, hydrogen, sulfide, and water, but instead it found only thin, hazy clouds. The probe detected only faint signs of lightning at least 600 miles (965 kilometers) away, far less than expected. It also discovered that lightning on Jupiter occurs only one-tenth as often as it does on Earth. Perhaps the biggest surprise uncovered by the probe was the lack of water on the planet.

The probe did not survive long enough to gather information on Jupiter's core. Astronomers believe the planet has a rocky core made of material similar to that of Earth's core. The temperature of the core may be as hot as 18,000°F (9,820°C), with pressures two million times those

Jupiter's Great Red Spot, a tremendous atmospheric storm twice the size of Earth, has been visible since the earliest observations of the planet with a telescope. The spot rotates counter-clockwise, completing a full rotation every six days. *(Reproduced by permission of National Aeronautics and Space Administration.)*

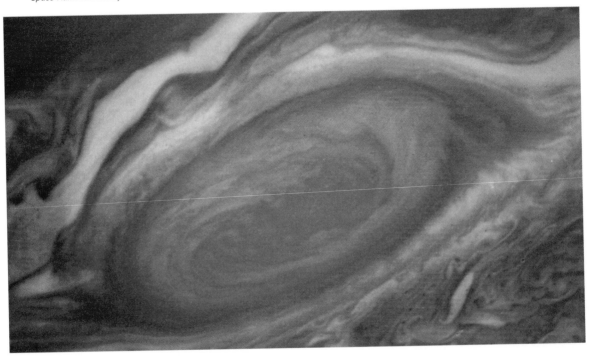

at Earth's surface. Scientists believe a layer of compressed hydrogen surrounds the core. Hydrogen in this layer may act like a metal and may be the cause of Jupiter's intense magnetic field (five times greater than the Sun's).

At the beginning of 2001, *Galileo* was still making valuable scientific observations about the planet and its moons, more than three years after its original two-year mission in orbit around Jupiter. The craft had already received three times the cumulative radiation exposure it was designed to withstand.

Comet Shoemaker-Levy 9 collides with Jupiter

In early 1993, Eugene Shoemaker (1928–1997), Carolyn Shoemaker (1948–), and David Levy discovered a comet moving across the night sky. They were surprised at its appearance, since it seemed elongated compared to other comets they had seen. Further observations showed that the comet consisted of a large number of fragments, apparently torn apart during a close encounter with Jupiter during a previous orbit. Calculations showed that this "string of pearls" would collide with Jupiter in July 1994.

A global effort was mounted to observe the impacts with nearly all ground-based and space-based telescopes available. Although astronomers could not predict what effect the collisions would have on Jupiter, or even whether they would be visible, the results turned out to be spectacular. Observatories around the world and satellite telescopes such as the Hubble Space Telescope observed the impacts and their effects. *Galileo,* en route to Jupiter at the time, provided astronomers with a front-row seat of the event. Even relatively small amateur telescopes were able to see some of the larger impact sites. Dark regions were visible in the atmosphere for months.

The data collected from the impact event will help scientists to understand the atmosphere of Jupiter, since the collisions dredged up material from parts of the atmosphere that are normally hidden. The wealth of information provided by *Galileo,* added to the Shoemaker-Levy impact data, is giving astronomers their best understanding yet of the biggest planet in our solar system.

[*See also* **Comet; Solar system; Space probe**]

Kangaroos and wallabies

Kangaroos and wallabies are pouched mammals, or marsupials, of Australia and nearby islands that are famous for their great leaping ability. The name kangaroo is usually used for large species and wallaby for smaller ones. They all belong to the family *Macropodidae*, meaning "big footed," and they are mainly herbivorous, or plant-eating. Most members of the family are nocturnal, feeding at night. Some live on the ground and some in trees. The largest kangaroo is the male red kangaroo, whose head and body can grow up to 6 feet (almost 2 meters) tall and tail to about 3.5 feet (1 meter) long. It can weigh 200 pounds (90 kilograms).

The two hind legs of kangaroos and wallabies are enlarged for leaping. The hind feet have four toes: two tiny ones used for grooming; a third, huge toe with a strong, sharp claw that can be used as a weapon; and another small toe. The kangaroo's two hands have five clawed fingers, all approximately the same length, used for grasping.

Kangaroos are often called "living pogo sticks"; indeed, the grey kangaroo has been known to jump up to 30 feet (over 9 meters) long and 6 feet (almost 2 meters) high. Because the springlike tendons in their hind legs store energy for leaps, it has been calculated that kangaroos actually use less energy hopping than a horse uses in running. A kangaroo tends to move in a leisurely fashion using all four feet plus its hefty tail for balance. Most are unable to walk moving their hind legs at separate times. They move their hind legs while balancing on the front legs and tail, then move the front legs while balancing on the hind legs, rather like a person walking on crutches. Tree-dwelling kangaroos do have the ability to move their hind legs at different times as they move among the branches.

Some kangaroos live in social groups and others are completely solitary. In general, the larger animals and the ones that live in open grasslands are more social. Within a group, called a mob, the individuals are safer. In a mob, the dominant male competes with the others to become the father of most of the offspring, called joeys. Because the dominant male is generally larger than the other males (called boomers), over many generations the males have become considerably larger than the females (called does).

The difficult life of a newborn kangaroo

For such a large animal, the gestation period (pregnancy) is incredibly short. The longest among the kangaroos is that of the eastern gray. The baby is born after only 38 days. It is less than an inch long, blind, and hairless like the newborns of all marsupials.

The kangaroo has virtually no hind legs at all when born. In fact, the front legs, which are clawed, look as if they are going to be mammoth. However, these relatively powerful front paws serve only the purpose of pulling the tiny unformed creature through its mother's fur and into her pouch, where her teats are located. (Like all marsupials, female kangaroos have a protective flap of fur-covered skin that shields the offspring as they suckle on teats. The kangaroo's marsupium, as this flap is called, is a full pouch that opens toward the head.) Once the baby's tiny mouth clamps onto a teat, the teat swells into the mouth so that the infant cannot release it. The baby, now called a pouch embryo, cannot let go even if it wants to. It will be a month or more before its jaw develops enough to open.

The pouch embryo will continue to develop as it would if it were inside a uterus (womb). Most of the big kangaroos will spend 10 months or more before the joey emerges for the first time (often falling out by accident). It gradually stays out for longer and longer periods, staying by its mother's side until it is about 18 months old. A male great kangaroo reaches sexual maturity at about two or three years, a female not for several years more.

The great kangaroos

One fossil kangaroo, *Procoptodon goliah,* was at least 10 feet (3 meters) tall and weighed about 500 pounds (227 kilograms). Today, the largest of the species is the male red kangaroo, which may have a head-and-body height of almost 6 feet (1.8 meters) with a tail about 3.5 feet (1 meter) long. It may weigh 200 pounds (90 kilograms).

Fourteen species of living kangaroos belong to the genus *Macropus*. Some of them are the largest marsupials. They have been regarded both as pests and as among the treasures of Australia. Farmers have long argued that they take food from sheep and cattle, but actually kangaroos select different grasses from the domestic livestock. Today, only a few are seen near urban areas, but they are widespread in the countryside, where they are still a favorite target of hunters, who sell their skins.

The eastern gray kangaroo and its western relative—which is actually brown in color—occupy the forest areas throughout the eastern half and the southwest region of the continent. In the continental interior, the red kangaroo lives in open dry land, while wallaroos, also called euros, live around rock outcroppings. The wallaroos, which have longer and shaggier hair than the larger kangaroos, are adapted for surviving with minimal water for nourishment. When water is not available, the animal reduces the body's need for it by hiding in cool rock shelters and their urinary systems concentrate the urine so that little liquid is lost.

Red kangaroos in Australia.
(Reproduced by permission of Photo Researchers, Inc.)

The smaller wallabies

Smaller kangaroos are usually called wallabies. The name is especially used for any kangaroo with a hind foot less than 10 inches (25 centimeters) long. The two smallest are the tammar wallaby of southwestern Australia and adjacent islands and the parma wallaby of New South Wales. Their heads and bodies are about 20 inches (50 centimeters) long with tails slightly longer. The tammar wallaby has been known to drink salt water. The whiptail wallaby is the most social of all marsupials. It lives in mobs of up to 50 individuals, and several mobs may occupy the same territory, making up an even bigger population.

Rock wallabies have soft fur that is usually colored to blend in with the dry, rocky surroundings in which they live. However, the yellow-footed rock wallaby is a colorful gray with a white strip on its face, yellow on its ears, dark down its back, yellow legs, and a ringed yellow-and-brown tail. Rock wallabies have thinner tails than other wallabies and use them only for balance, not for propping themselves up. They are very agile moving among the rocks. Some have been known to leap straight up a rock face 13 feet (4 meters) or more. Rock wallabies have sometimes been let loose in zoos, where they live and breed in communal groups.

Several wallabies that were widespread in the past are probably already extinct. Called nail-tailed wallabies, they have tough, horny tips to their tails. These 2-foot-high (60-centimeter) marsupials lost their habitat to grazing livestock and farms. Nail-tails have been called "organ grinders" because their forearms rotate while they are hopping.

Tree kangaroos

The tree kangaroos live in trees high on the mountainsides of New Guinea and Australia. They have fairly long fur and live in small groups. Some of them have the ability to leap between strong branches of trees as much as 30 feet (9 meters) apart.

Tree kangaroos have longer forearms and longer tails than land-dwelling kangaroos. Although their tails are not truly prehensile, or grasping, they may wrap themselves around a branch to help support them. Unlike other kangaroos, their tails are the same thickness from base to tip. Tree kangaroos are often hunted and so are decreasing in numbers. This decrease is augmented by the fact that the single young stays in the pouch for almost a year and suckles even longer.

Disappearing rat-kangaroos

A subfamily of smaller, more primitive marsupials are called rat-kangaroos. These animals tend to be omnivorous, eating a variety of foods.

The musky rat-kangaroo is the smallest member of the kangaroo family, with a head-body length of only about 10 inches (25 centimeters) high plus a furless tail (the only one in the family) about 5 inches (12 centimeters) long. This species also has front and hind feet closer to the same size than any other member of the family. It eats some insects along with its grasses.

The bettong, also called the woylie or brush-tailed rat-kangaroo, has a prehensile tail, which it uses to carry the dry grasses used in building a nest. Woylies were quite common over southern Australia, but as human populations have increased, it has become extinct in most of its range. Similarly threatened is the boodie or short-nosed rat-kangaroo. The only kangaroo that digs burrows, in which it gathers in a family group, it is now restricted to several islands in western Australia's Shark Bay. Unlike the other members of the kangaroo family, the boodie never uses its front feet while walking.

Clearly, many of the smaller members of the kangaroo are threatened or even nearing extinction. Apparently, they are more vulnerable to even the smallest changes in their habitats. The great kangaroos, on the other hand, appear to be thriving as long as their habitats remain protected and hunting for their skins is kept at a minimum.

L

Lake

Lakes are inland bodies of standing water. Although millions of lakes are scattered over Earth's surface, most are located in higher latitudes and mountainous areas. Canada alone contains almost 50 percent of the world's lakes. Lakes can be formed by glaciers, tectonic plate movements, river and wind currents, and volcanic or meteorite activity. Some lakes are only seasonal, drying up during parts of the year.

The study of lakes, ponds, and other freshwater bodies is called limnology (pronounced lim-NOL-o-gee). Although ponds are considered small, shallow lakes, there is one important difference between the two bodies of water: temperature. Ponds generally have a consistent temperature throughout, whereas lakes have various temperature layers, depending on the season.

The Great Lakes of the United States and Canada are the world's largest system of freshwater lakes. Lake Superior, the northernmost of the Great Lakes, is the world's largest freshwater lake with an area of 31,820 square miles (82,730 square kilometers). Lake Titicaca in the Andes Mountains on the border between Peru and Bolivia is the world's highest large freshwater lake at 12,500 feet (3,800 meters) above sea level.

Some freshwater lakes become salty over time, especially in arid regions. Because the water in these lakes evaporates quickly, the salt from inflowing waters reaches a high concentration. Among the world's greatest salt lakes are the Caspian Sea, Dead Sea, and Great Salt Lake. Covering an area of about 144,000 square miles (372,960 square kilometers), the Caspian Sea is the largest lake in the world. At 1,292 feet (394 meters) below sea level, the Dead Sea is the lowest lake in the world.

▼ **Words to Know**

Blowout: Lake basin created in coastal or arid region by strong winds shifting sand.

Caldera: Volcanic crater that has collapsed to form a depression greater than 1 mile (1.6 kilometers) in diameter.

Eutrophication: Natural process by which a lake or other body of water becomes enriched in dissolved nutrients, spurring aquatic plant growth.

Limnology: Study of lakes, ponds, and other freshwater bodies.

Oxbow lake: Lake created when a loop of a river is separated from the main flow by gravel, sand, and silt deposits.

Solution lake: Lake created when groundwater erodes bedrock, resulting in a sinkhole.

Turnover: Mixing and flip-flopping of the differing temperature layers within a lake.

Origins of lakes

Most lakes on Earth were formed as a result of glacier activity. Earth's glacial ice formed and extended into what is now Canada, the northernmost United States, and northern Europe. As the heavy, thick ice pushed along, it created crevices by scouring out topsoil and even carving into bedrock (the solid rock that lies beneath the soil). Glacial growth peaked about 20,000 years ago, after which time the ice slowly began to melt. As the ice melted, the glaciers retreated, but the basins formed by glaciers remained and filled with water from the melting glaciers.

Movements of Earth's crust, water, and wind can also form lakes. The moving of the plates that compose Earth's crust (called tectonic activity) often forms basins, especially along fault lines (where plates meet and move against each other). These basins or depressions fill with water, forming lakes such as Lake Baikal in Siberia.

Water currents and land erosion by water form oxbow and solution lakes. Oxbow lakes are created when winding rivers such as the Mississippi change course, carrying water through twists and turns that form loops. As deposits build up and separate a loop from the main flow of the river, an oxbow lake such as Lake Whittington in Mississippi forms. Solution lakes result from groundwater eroding the bedrock above it, creating a sinkhole. Lakes from sinkholes are the predominant type in Florida and on Mexico's Yucatan Peninsula. Wind can also create lake basins called blowouts, which usually occur in coastal or arid regions. Blowouts created by shifted sand are typical in northern Texas, New Mexico, southern Africa, and parts of Australia.

A few lakes are formed by volcanic activity or meteors. After erupting, some volcanoes collapse, forming basins that collect water. Volcanic basins with diameters greater than one mile are called calderas. Crater Lake in Oregon (the seventh deepest lake in the world) is a caldera 1,932 feet (590 meters) deep, 6 miles (10 kilometers) long, and 5 miles (8 kilometers) wide. The largest meteorite-formed lake in the world is found in New Quebec Crater (formerly Chubb Crater) in northern Quebec, Canada. It is 823 feet (250 meters) deep inside a crater about 2 miles (3 kilometers) wide.

Water circulation

Water circulation is the mixing of water in a lake. When the three temperature layers of a lake mix and change places, a lake is said to un-

Kettle lakes like this one in Dundee, Wisconsin, are formed when blocks of ice buried by moving glaciers melt and leave a depression. *(Reproduced by permission of JLM Visuals.)*

dergo turnover. Turnover occurs when water in an upper layer is denser, or heavier, than the layer of water underneath it. Cooler water tends to be denser than warmer water. Deeper water is generally both denser and colder than shallow water.

In autumn, the upper layers of a lake cool down because of the cooling air above. Eventually, these layers, mixed by winds, cool to a temperature lower than that of the layer at the bottom of the lake. When this occurs, the lowest layer rises to the surface, mixing with the other layers. This process is called fall turnover.

Rocky shore of Lake Huron, one of the Great Lakes and the world's fifth largest. (Reproduced by permission of Field Mark Publications.)

In spring, ice covering a lake melts and mixes with the upper layer, which then becomes denser than the layers beneath. Mixing takes place and the whole lake turns over. This is spring turnover.

Lake threats

Pollution is the major threat to the life of a lake. Acid rain is formed by sulfates and nitrates emitted from coal-burning industries and automobile exhaust pipes. These chemicals combine with moisture and sunlight in the atmosphere to form sulfuric and nitric acids that enter lakes via rain and other precipitation. Acid rain is 10 times more acidic than normal rain. When a freshwater lake becomes too acidic, its life-forms gradually die. Other chemical pollutants include fertilizers and pesticides, which enter lakes through soil run-offs into streams. Pesticides are toxic to fish, while fertilizers can cause eutrophication (pronounced YOU-tro-fi-KAY-shun).

Eutrophication is the natural process by which a lake or other body of water becomes enriched in dissolved nutrients (such as nitrogen and phosphorus) that spur aquatic plant growth. Increased plant growth leads to an increase in the organic remains on the bottom of a lake. Over time, perhaps centuries, the remains build up, the lake becomes shallower, and plants take root. Finally, as plant life fills in the water basin, the lake turns into a marsh and then a meadow.

Chemical pollutants, including phosphorous and nitrogen compounds, can artificially accelerate this aging process. The growth of algae and other plant life is overstimulated, and they quickly consume most of the dissolved oxygen in the water. Soon, the lake's oxygen supply is fully depleted and all life in it dies.

[*See also* **Eutrophication; Ice ages; River; Water**]

Lanthanides

The lanthanides are the chemical elements found in Row 6 of the periodic table between Groups 3 and 4. They follow lanthanum (La), element #57, which accounts for their family name. The lanthanides include the metals cerium (Ce), praseodymium (Pr), neodymium (Nd), promethium (Pm), samarium (Sm), europium (Eu), gadolinium (Gd), terbium (Tb), dysprosium (Dy), holmium (Ho), erbium (Er), thulium (Tm), ytterbium (Yb), and lutetium (Lu).

▼ Words to Know

Alloy: A mixture of two or more metals with properties different from those of the metals of which it is made.

Catalyst: A material that speeds up the rate of a reaction without undergoing any change in its own composition.

Monazite: A mineral that constitutes the major source of the lanthanides.

Oxide: A compound containing oxygen and one other element.

Phosphor: A substance that glows when struck by electrons.

Rare earth elements: An older name for the lanthanide elements.

Lanthanides as rare earth elements

At one time, the lanthanides were called the rare earth elements. The name suggests that chemists once thought that the elements were present in Earth's crust in only very small amounts. As it turns out, with one exception, that assumption was not correct. (That exception is promethium, which was first discovered in the products of a nuclear fission reaction in 1945. Very small amounts of promethium have also been found in naturally occurring ores of uranium.)

The other lanthanides are relatively abundant in Earth's crust. Cerium, for example, is the twenty-sixth most abundant element. Even thulium, the second rarest lanthanide after promethium, is more abundant than iodine.

The point of interest about the lanthanides, then, is not that they are so rare, but that they are so much alike. Most of the lanthanides occur together in nature, and they are very difficult to separate from each other. Indeed, the discovery of the lanthanide elements is one of the most intriguing detective stories in all of chemistry. That story includes episodes in which one element was thought to be another, two elements were identified as one, some elements were mistakenly identified, and so on. By 1907, however, the confusion had been sorted out, and all of the lanthanides (except promethium) had been identified.

Occurrence

The most important source of the lanthanides is monazite, a heavy dark sand found in Brazil, India, Australia, South Africa, and the United

States. The composition of monazite varies depending on its location, but it generally contains about 50 percent of lanthanide compounds by weight. Because of the similarity of their properties and their occurrence together in nature, the lanthanides can be separated from each other and purified only with considerable effort. Consequently, commercial production of the lanthanides tends to be expensive.

Properties

Like most metals, the lanthanides have a bright silvery appearance. Five of the elements (lanthanum, cerium, praseodymium, neodymium, and europium) are very reactive. When exposed to air, they react with oxygen to form an oxide coating that tarnishes the surface. For this reason these metals are stored under mineral oil. The remainder of the lanthanides are not as reactive, and some (gadolinium and lutetium) retain their silvery metallic appearance for a long time.

When contaminated with nonmetals, such as oxygen or nitrogen, the lanthanides become brittle. They also corrode more easily if contaminated with other metals, such as calcium. Their melting points range from about 819°C (1,506°F) for ytterbium to about 1,663°C (3,025°F) for lutetium. The lanthanides form alloys (mixtures) with many other metals, and these alloys exhibit a wide range of physical properties.

The lanthanides react slowly with cold water and more rapidly with hot water to form hydrogen gas. They burn readily in air to form oxides. They also form compounds with many nonmetals, such as hydrogen, fluorine, phosphorous, sulfur, and chlorine.

Uses of lanthanides

Until fairly recently, the lanthanides had relatively few applications; they cost so much to produce that less expensive alternatives were usually available. The best known lanthanide alloy, Auer metal, is a mixture of cerium and iron that produces a spark when struck. It has long been used as a flint in cigarette and gas lighters. Auer metal is one of a series of mixed lanthanide alloys known as misch metals. The misch metals are composed of varying amounts of the lanthanide metals, mostly cerium and smaller amounts of others such as lanthanum, neodymium, and praseodymium. They have been used to impart strength, hardness, and inertness to structural materials. They have also been used to remove oxygen and sulfur impurities from various industrial systems.

In recent years, less expensive methods have been developed for the production of the lanthanides. As a result, they are now used in a greater variety of applications. One such application is as catalysts, substances that speed up chemical reactions. In the refining industry, for example, the lanthanides are used as catalysts in the conversion of crude oil into gasoline, kerosene, diesel and heating oil, and other products.

The lanthanides are also used as phosphors in color television sets. Phosphors are chemicals that glow with various colors when struck by electrons. For example, oxides of europium and yttrium are used to produce the red colors on a television screen. Other lanthanide compounds are used in streetlights, searchlights, and in the high-intensity lighting present in sports stadiums.

The ceramics industry uses lanthanide oxides to color ceramics and glasses. Optical lenses made with lanthanum oxide are used in cameras and binoculars. Compounds of praseodymium and neodymium are used in glass, such as in television screens, to reduce glare. Cerium oxide has been used to polish glass.

The lanthanides also have a variety of nuclear applications. Because they absorb neutrons, they have been employed in control rods used to regulate nuclear reactors. They have also been used as shielding materials and as structural components in reactors. Some lanthanides have unusual magnetic properties. For instance, cobalt-samarium magnets are very strong permanent magnets.

[*See also* **Element, chemical; Periodic table**]

Laser

A laser is a device used to create a narrow, intense beam of very bright light. Laser stands for Light Amplification by Stimulated Emission of Radiation. The light emitted by a laser, either visible light or invisible infrared light, differs from the light emitted by a normal lightbulb in three ways. First, laser light is highly concentrated and moves in a particular direction. Normal light is emitted from its source in all directions. Second, laser light is composed of a single color or wavelength. Third, laser light is coherent, meaning all its light waves are synchronized (vibrating in exactly the same way). These combined properties allow laser light to transmit large amounts of energy or information over a great distance.

How it works

To produce laser light, energy is pumped into a medium, which may be a solid (such as a ruby crystal), a liquid, or a gas. This energy, either

Words to Know

Absorption band: Measurement in terms of wavelengths in which a material such as living tissue will absorb the energy of laser light.

Coherent light: Light beam where the component wavelengths are synchronous or all in step with each other.

Photon: Light particle emitted by an atom as excess energy when that atom returns from an excited state (high energy) to its normal state.

Stimulated emission: Process of emitting light in which one photon stimulates the generation of a second photon which is identical in all respects to the first.

light, heat, or electricity, excites the atoms in the medium, raising them to a high-energy state. As an excited atom returns to its original state, it rids itself of excess energy by giving off a photon, or particle of light. This photon then goes on to strike another excited atom, causing it to release an identical photon. This second photon, in turn, strikes another excited atom, causing the release of yet another identical photon. This chain reaction is called stimulated emission.

Two precisely aligned mirrors at each end of the laser material cause the released photons to move back and forth, repeating the striking process millions of times. As each photon is released, its wavelength is synchronous or in step with that of every other photon. As this light builds up, it passes through one end-mirror, which is slightly transparent.

Uses of the laser

In medicine, lasers have been used to perform very delicate surgeries. They are extremely useful because the wavelengths produced by lasers can be matched to a specific body part's ability to absorb the light (known as its absorption band). Since different tissues and cells have different absorption bands, the laser will only vaporize the tissue whose absorption band matches the wavelength of that particular laser light.

In a relatively short procedure that requires no anesthetic, lasers are used to correct detached retinas and other visual impairments. Lasers are also used to remove birthmarks and tattoos from the skin, seal blood vessels during operations to prevent bleeding, and reopen arteries blocked by fatty deposits.

Since a laser beam can be focused down to a very small spot of light, its energy can be extremely dense. When focused on a material such as metal, an infrared laser beam can raise the surface temperature up to 9,032°F (5,000°C). For this reason, lasers are used for the precise cutting of metals, such as drilling long thin holes or cutting complex shapes quickly.

Lasers are also utilized in communications, where a tube of fiber optic material can be used to transmit a beam of uninterrupted laser light over long distances. Supermarkets use helium-neon lasers in checkout lanes to scan price codes. Perhaps the most familiar use of the laser is in compact disc players. Aluminum discs containing audio or visual information are encased in clear plastic. The laser beam then "reads" the information through the plastic without touching the surface and transfers that information to speakers or video screens.

A laser beam is reflected off mirrors and through filters at Colorado State University. (Reproduced by permission of The Stock Market.)

[*See also* **Compact disc; Fiber optics; Hologram and holography**]

Laws of motion

The term laws of motion generally refers to three statements originally devised by English physicist Isaac Newton (1642–1727) in the 1680s. These laws, along with Newton's law of gravitation, are generally considered to be the ultimate solution to a problem that had troubled scholars for more than 2,000 years: motion.

History

Examples of motion are everywhere in the world around us. What makes a rock fall off a cliff? How does a skate slide across an icy surface? What keeps the planets in their orbits around the Sun? It is only natural, then, that questions about motion were foremost in the minds of ancient philosophers and physicists.

Greek philosopher Aristotle (384–322 B.C.), for example, tried to find the causes of motion. He said that some forms of motion were "natural." Rocks fall toward the ground because the ground is a natural place for rocks to be. Objects rise into the air when they are heated because the Sun is hot, and so it is natural for heat to rise.

Aristotle classified other forms of motion as "violent" because they were not natural to his way of thinking. For example, shooting an arrow through space produced violent motion since the arrow's natural tendency was to fall straight down toward Earth.

Aristotle's thinking about motion dominated Western thought for 2,000 years. Unfortunately, his ideas were not really very productive, and scholars tried continually to improve on the concepts of natural and violent motion—without much success.

Then, in the early seventeenth century, Italian astronomer and physicist Galileo Galilei (1564–1642) proposed a whole new way of looking at the problem of motion. Since asking *why* things move had not been very productive, Galileo said, perhaps physicists should focus simply on describing *how* they move. A whole new philosophy of physics (the science of matter and energy) was created and, in the process, the science of physics itself was born.

Newton's three laws

Newton, who was born in the year that Galileo died, produced a nearly perfect (for the time) response to Galileo's suggestion. He said that

Words to Know

Acceleration: The rate at which the velocity of an object changes with time.

Force: A physical interaction (pushing or pulling) tending to change the state of motion (velocity) of an object.

Inertia: The tendency of an object to continue in its state of motion.

Mass: A measure of an amount of matter.

Velocity: The rate at which the position of an object changes with time, including both the speed and the direction.

the movement of objects can be fully described in only three laws. These laws all show how motion is related to forces. One definition for the term force in science is a push or a pull. If you push a wooden block across the top of a table, for example, you exert a force on the block. One benefit of Newton's laws is that they provide an even more precise definition for force, as will be demonstrated later.

The first law. Newton's first law of motion is that an object tends to continue in its motion at a constant velocity until and unless an outside force acts on it. The term velocity refers both to the speed and the direction in which an object is moving.

For example, suppose that you shoot an arrow into space. Newton's first law says that the arrow will continue moving in the direction you aimed it at its original speed until and unless some outside force acts on it. The main outside forces acting on an arrow are friction from air and gravity.

As the arrow continues to move, it will slow down. The arrow is passing through air, whose molecules rub against the arrow, causing it to lose speed. In addition, the arrow begins to change direction, moving toward Earth because of gravitational forces. If you could imagine shooting an arrow into the near-perfect vacuum of outer space, the arrow would continue moving in the same direction at the same speed forever. With no air present—and beyond the range of Earth's gravitational attraction—the arrow's motion would not change.

The first law also applies to objects at rest. An object at rest is simply an object whose velocity is zero. The object will continue to remain at rest until and unless a force acts on it. For example, a person might hit the object with a mallet. The force of the blow might change the object's motion, giving it both speed and direction.

The property of objects described by the first law is known as inertia. The term inertia simply means that objects tend to continue in whatever their state of motion is. If moving, they continue to move in the same way, or, if at rest, they continue to remain at rest unless acted on by an outside force.

The second law. Newton's second law clearly states the relationship between motion and force. Mathematically, the law can be stated as $F = m \cdot a$, where F represents the force exerted on an object, m is the object's mass, and a is the acceleration given to the object. The term acceleration means how fast the velocity of an object is changing and in what direction.

To understand the second law, think of a soccer ball sitting on the ground. If you kick that ball with a certain force, the ball will be given a certain acceleration. If you kick the ball with twice the force, the ball will be given twice the acceleration. If the ball then bounces off the goal post and out of bounds, the force of the impact with the goal post will change the ball's direction.

The second law provides a more precise way of defining force. Force is any action that causes a body to change the speed or direction with which it is moving.

The third law. Newton's third law says that for every action there is an equal and opposite reaction. A simple example of the law is a rocket. A rocket is simply a cylindrical device closed at one end and open at the other end in which a fuel is burned. As the fuel burns, hot gases are formed and released through the open end of the rocket. The escape of the gases in one direction can be considered as an action. Newton's law says that this action must be balanced by a second action that is equal in magnitude and opposite in direction. That opposite action is the movement of the rocket in a direction opposite that of the escaping gases. That is, the gases go out the back of the rocket (the action), while the rocket itself moves forward (the reaction).

[*See also* **Acceleration; Celestial mechanics; Gravity and gravitation; Mass**]

Leaf

A leaf is a plant's principal organ of photosynthesis, the process by which sunlight is used to form foods from carbon dioxide and water. Leaves also help in the process of transpiration, or the loss of water vapor from a plant.

A typical leaf is an outgrowth of a stem and has two main parts: the blade (flattened portion) and the petiole (pronounced PET-ee-ole; the stalk connecting the blade to the stem). Some leaves also have stipules, small

Bay laurel leaves. *(Reproduced by permission of Field Mark Publications.)*

Words to Know

Abscission layer: Barrier of special cells created at the base of petioles in autumn.

Blade: Flattened part of a leaf.

Chloroplasts: Small structures that contain chlorophyll and in which the process of photosynthesis takes place.

Margin: Outer edge of a blade.

Midrib: Single main vein running down the center of a blade.

Petiole: Stalk connecting the blade of a leaf to the stem.

Phloem: Plant tissue consisting of elongated cells that transport carbohydrates and other nutrients.

Photosynthesis: Process by which a plant uses sunlight to form foods from carbon dioxide and water.

Stomata: Pores in the epidermis of leaves.

Transpiration: Evaporation of water in the form of water vapor from the stomata.

Xylem: Plant tissue consisting of elongated cells that transport water and mineral nutrients.

paired outgrowths at the base of the petiole. Scientists are not quite sure of the function of stipules.

Leaf size and shape differ widely among different species of plants. Duckweeds are tiny aquatic plants with leaves that are less than 0.04 inch (1 millimeter) in diameter, the smallest of any plant species. Certain species of palm trees have the largest known leaves, more than 230 feet (70 meters) in length.

Leaf arrangement

A leaf can be classified as simple or compound according to its arrangement. A simple leaf has a single blade. A compound leaf consists of two or more separate blades, each of which is termed a leaflet. Each leaflet can be borne at one point or at intervals on each side of a stalk. Compound leaves with leaflets originating from the same point on the petiole (like fingers of an outstretched hand) are called palmately compound. Compound leaves with leaflets originating from different points along a central stalk are called pinnately compound.

All leaves, no matter their shape, are attached to the stem in one of three ways: opposite, alternate, or whorled. Opposite leaves are those growing in pairs opposite or across from each other on the stem. Alternate leaves are attached on alternate sides of the stem. Whorled leaves are three or more leaves growing around the stem at the same spot. Most plant species have alternate leaves.

Blade

The outer edge of a blade is called the margin. An entire margin is one that is smooth and has no indentations. A toothed margin has small or wavy indentations. A lobed margin has large indentations (called sinuses) and large projections (called lobes).

A scanning electron micrograph of open stomata on the underside of a rose leaf. Stomata are breathing pores scattered over the leaf surface that regulate the exchange of gases between the leaf's interior and the atmosphere. *(Reproduced by permission of Photo Researchers, Inc.)*

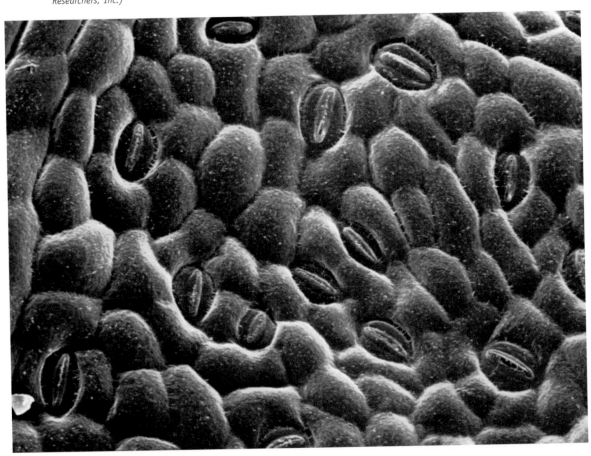

Venation is the pattern of veins in the blade of a leaf. A single main vein running down the center of a blade is called a midrib. Several main veins are referred to as principle veins. A network of smaller veins branch off from a midrib or a principle vein.

All veins transport nutrients and water in and out of the leaves. The two primary tissues in leaf veins are xylem (pronounced ZY-lem) and phloem (pronounced FLOW-em). Xylem cells mainly transport water and mineral nutrients from the roots to the leaves. Phloem cells mainly transport carbohydrates (made by photosynthesis) from the leaves to the rest of the plant. Typically, xylem cells are on the upper side of the leaf vein and phloem cells are on the lower side.

Internal anatomy of leaves

Although the leaves of different plants vary in their overall shape, most leaves are rather similar in their internal anatomy. Leaves generally consist of epidermal tissue on the upper and lower surfaces and mesophyll tissue throughout the body.

Epidermal cells have two features that prevent the plant from losing water: they are packed densely together and they are covered by a cuticle (a waxy layer secreted by the cells). The epidermis usually consists of a single layer of cells, although the specialized leaves of some desert plants have epidermal layers that are several cells thick. The epidermis contains small pores called stomata, which are mostly found on the lower leaf surface. Each individual stoma (pore) is surrounded by a pair of specialized guard cells. In most species, the guard cells close their stomata during the night (and during times of drought) to prevent water loss. During the day, the guard cells open their stomata so they can take in carbon dioxide for photosynthesis and give off oxygen as a waste product.

The mesophyll layer is divided into two parts: palisade cells and spongy cells. Palisade cells are densely packed, elongated cells lying directly beneath the upper epidermis. These cells house chloroplasts, small structures that contain chlorophyll and in which the process of photosynthesis takes place. Spongy cells are large, often odd-shaped cells lying underneath palisade cells. They are loosely packed to allow gases (carbon dioxide, oxygen, and water vapor) to move freely between them.

Leaves in autumn

Leaves are green in summer because they contain the pigment chlorophyll, which absorbs all the wavelengths of sunlight except for green (sunlight or white light comprises all the colors of the visible spectrum: red, orange, yellow, green, blue, indigo, and violet). In addition to chlorophyll, leaves contain carotenoid (pronounced kuh-ROT-in-oid) pigments, which appear orange-yellow. In autumn, plants create a barrier of special cells, called the abscission (pronounced ab-SI-zhen) layer, at the base of the petiole. Moisture and nutrients from the plant are cut off and the leaf begins to die. Chlorophyll is very unstable and begins to break down quickly. The carotenoid pigments, which are more stable, remain in the leaf after the chlorophyll has faded, giving the plant a vibrant yellow or gold appearance.

The red autumn color of certain plants comes from a purple-red pigment known as anthocyanin (pronounced an-tho-SIGH-a-nin). Unlike carotenoids, anthocyanins are not present in a leaf during the summer. They are produced only after a leaf starts to die. During the autumn cycle of warm days and cool nights, sugars remaining in the leaf undergo a chemical reaction, producing anthocyanins.

[*See also* **Photosynthesis**]

LED (light-emitting diode)

An LED, or light-emitting diode, is a special type of diode that emits light when connected in a circuit. A diode is an electronic device that has two electrodes arranged in such a manner as to allow electrical current to flow in one direction only. With its ability to control the flow of electrons, a diode is often used as a rectifier, which is a device that converts alternating current into direct current. Alternating current is an electric current that flows first in one direction and then in the other. Since alternating current fed into a diode can move in one direction only, the diode converts the current to a one-way flow known as a direct current.

An LED converts electrical energy to light by means of a semiconductor, a substance that conducts an electric current, but only very poorly. A semiconductor for an LED is made from an extremely thin slice of crystal. A clear (or often colored) epoxy case encloses the semiconductor. Two leads extend down below the epoxy enclosure.

The semiconductor has two regions—*p* and *n*—separated by a junction. The *p* region is dominated by positive electric charges; the *n* region is dominated by negative electric charges (electrons). The junction acts as a barrier to the flow of electrons between the *p* and the *n* regions. Only

Words to Know

Diode: Electronic device that allows current to flow in one direction only.

Rectifier: Device that converts alternating current (AC) to direct current (DC).

Semiconductor: Substance, such as silicon or germanium, whose ability to carry electrical current is lower than that of a conductor (like metal) and higher than that of insulators (like rubber).

when sufficient voltage is applied to the semiconductor can the current flow, and the electrons cross the junction into the *p* region.

Circuit board with red and green light-emitting diode (LED) indicator lights from a radar detector. *(Reproduced by permission of The Stock Market.)*

When electric current is applied to the semiconductor across the leads of the LED, electrons can move easily in only one direction across the junction between the p and n regions. Once the current starts to flow, electrons in the n region have sufficient energy to move across the junction into the p region. Once in the p region, the electrons are immediately attracted to the positive charges. When an electron moves sufficiently close to a positive charge in the p region, the two charges "recombine." In order to return to its low-energy position after recombining with a positive charge, an electron must shed the energy it picked up from the cur-

This light-emitting diode (LED) uses a semiconductor to control the flow of electrons. *(Reproduced by permission of Phototake.)*

rent in the form of photons, which emit visible light. This is the light produced by an LED.

The color produced by an LED is dependent on the material composing its semiconductor. Early LEDs emitted only red light. Green and amber LEDs were introduced next. By the mid 1990s, blue and white LEDs had been developed.

Convenient uses

LEDs are commonly used as indicator lights. They are found in electronic toys, computers, calculators, telephones, and many other household devices. They are immune to electromagnetic interference, power surge hazards, and changes in temperature. Because they are a completely cool light source, LEDs are much more efficient than standard incandescent lightbulbs that give off a lot of energy in the form of infrared radiation (heat). In comparison, LEDs are often up to ten times more efficient.

Many cities in the United States are replacing their incandescent traffic lights with LED units (hundreds of LEDs in an array) because the LED units are brighter (they have equal brightness across their entire surface), they last longer (years versus months), and they are much more energy efficient.

[See also **Diode**]

Legionnaires' disease

Legionnaires' disease is an acute respiratory infection caused by a common bacteria that results in a serious case of pneumonia. It first became a well-known disease in 1976 when a serious outbreak occurred among a large number of people attending an American Legion convention. Researchers eventually discovered that the bacteria can be easily found in nature wherever there is warm and moist stagnant water, and that it is transmitted by breathing it in.

A mysterious outbreak

During July 21 to 24, 1976, over 4,000 members of the American Legion met in Philadelphia, Pennsylvania, to attend their fifty-eighth annual convention and to celebrate the nation's two hundredth birthday. When the meetings were over, the attendees and their families returned home, but not all was right. On July 27, only three days after the convention, one

Words to Know

Antibody: A protein produced by certain cells of the body as an immune (disease-fighting) response to a specific foreign antigen, or any substance that the body considers foreign, such as a bacterial cell.

Bacteria: Single-celled microorganisms that live in soil, water, plants, and animals that play a key role in the decay of organic matter and the cycling of nutrients. Some are agents of disease.

Pneumonia: Any of several diseases caused by bacteria or viruses in which the lungs become inflamed.

of the legionnaires who had been in Philadelphia died from a pneumonia-like illness. On July 30, a physician in Bloomsburg, Pennsylvania, realized that the three patients he was treating for a similar condition had all attended the convention in Philadelphia. That same day, a nurse in the nearby Chambersburg Hospital noted a similar condition in three patients who had gone to the same convention. However, it was not until August 2 that state officials were able to put together the illness with its victims' whereabouts and to realize that there was some undeniable connection between this serious febrile (pronounced FEH-brile) or feverish illness and the legionnaires' convention. By that date, eighteen legionnaires had already died. Federal officials at the Center for Disease Control (CDC) were notified and became immediately involved in what was now a mysterious and spreading outbreak.

"Philly Killer"

By this time the media realized that it had a major story on its hands, and from then on health officials had to work under the close watch of radio, television, and newspaper reporters. Still, no one, including the CDC, was able to pinpoint the immediate cause of this disease. Since it was now directly connected to the Philadelphia legionnaires' convention, the media referred to it as the "Philly Killer," "Legion Malady," "Legion Fever," "Legion Disease," and finally the name that took hold, "Legionnaires' disease." As this name became used regularly, some members of the American Legion thought it was bad for the organization since it might suggest that they were somehow responsible for the disease. Other members thought the opposite and considered it a sort of tribute or honor to those who had already died. Despite their opinions, the name for the disease stuck, and it is still called that today by non-scientists.

Probably the main reason for the name sticking was that researchers could not identify the organism causing this disease and therefore had nothing to name it. Technically, the CDC simply called it "Respiratory Infection-Pennsylvania." For several months as they studied the disease, this name persisted until an April 1977 CDC report made reference to "Legionnaires' disease." From then on, even after the bacterium that caused the disease was identified and named, the press and even some in the medical community would refer to it by its popular name.

Discovery by CDC

It was not until nearly six months after the first outbreak that the cause of this disease was identified positively by the CDC. On January 18, 1977, the CDC announced that their investigators had isolated the cause of Legionnaires' disease. Using a piece of lung tissue taken from one of its dead victims, researchers finally were able to demonstrate that a bacterium they would name *Legionella pneumophila* (pronounced lee-juh-NELL-uh new-mo-FEE-lee-uh) was the culprit. By then however, a total of 221 people had contracted the disease and 34 of them had died. Isolating the actual bacterium enabled the CDC not only to learn how it had spread and how to fight it, but it showed researchers that this was a complicated organism responsible for many past unexplained outbreaks.

Course of disease

The *Legionella* bacterium was an unusual and complicated germ because it was found to cause two diseases, one very serious known as Legionnaires' disease and another milder form called Pontiac Fever. Although Pontiac Fever is caught by 95 percent of the people exposed to it, most of them simply experience flulike symptoms that pass in two to five days. Legionnaires' disease is much harder to catch, with only two to five percent of those exposed actually contracting it. But once contracted, usually by at-risk individuals who are more susceptible, it will not go away without medication and it kills between five and fifteen percent of the people it infects.

Source of infection

CDC researchers named the species of bacteria *Legionella pneumophila* because the second word means "lung-loving" in Latin. This bacteria is actually very common in the natural world and only causes trouble when it gets into people's respiratory systems. It finds our lungs to be an especially comfortable place because they have conditions the bacteria prefer—they are warm and moist. *Legionella* are found to exist naturally in stagnant water, and in the Philadelphia case, the CDC traced the outbreak source to the hotel's air conditioning system whose condenser was vented very close to its air intake system. This meant that the large air conditioning system, which had not been cleaned for some time, had the common *Legionella* germ growing in it, which people then inhaled after the organism had gotten into the air intake pipes.

Attacks the susceptible

The fact that this is the only way that people can contract the disease was discovered by the CDC. Unlike many diseases, you cannot "catch" this disease from another person. The *Legionella* germ must penetrate deep into the lungs. Further, the cilia (pronounced SIL-lee-uh) in most people's lungs usually capture and expel the bacteria. However, for those who are somehow at risk—like smokers, alcoholics, older people with chronic lung problems, or someone with a weak immune system—these short hairlike projections called cilia do not work the way they should. The *Legionella* can then get in and infect a person. Another un-

Legionalla pneomophila.
(Reproduced by permission of Custom Medical Stock Photo, Inc.)

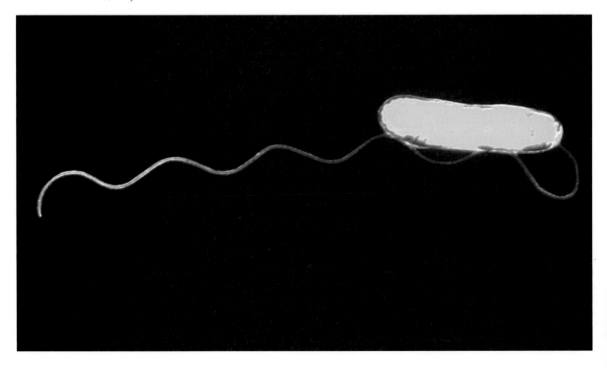

usual thing about this disease is that the infecting bacteria invade the body's white blood cells and multiply inside them. These are the very cells that the body uses to fight such invaders. Normally, these attack white cells called phagocytes (pronounced FA-go-sites) surround and engulf or swallow up a bacterial invader. Although the phagocytes do manage to engulf the *Legionella*, they are unable to digest it and soon the attacker becomes the attacked. In fact, the *Legionella* becomes a parasite and actually begins multiplying inside the phagocyte, who now becomes its host. After doubling its numbers every two hours, the *Legionella* eventually overloads its host, which bursts and spreads even more invading cells throughout the body. The CDC discovered that the antibiotic erythromycin (pronounced eh-RI-throw-MY-sin) is effective. However, it works not by killing the bacteria but rather by stopping it from multiplying in the cells, therefore giving the body a good chance to combat it on its own.

A new "old" disease

Once the real cause of the disease was known and well understood, researchers realized that this was not some new bacterium that had suddenly emerged but one that had been around all the time. It was simply one that science had never identified. With hindsight, they found that an estimated 8,000 to 18,000 people get some form of Legionnaires' disease every year in the United States. Further, they found that the disease occurs worldwide. For example, it is so common in Australia that roughly one-third of the population has antibodies for it in their blood (meaning that they have been exposed to it at some point in their lives and their bodies have developed a way to combat it).

Since *Legionella* has been found in cooling towers and evaporative condensers of large air conditioning systems, as well as in spas and showers, all of which have temperature conditions that allow it to thrive, it is important to keep these systems clean and well-maintained. *Legionella* is easily killed by heating water to high temperatures. It dies off quickly if it dries out and it is also killed by simple exposure to the ultraviolet radiation of the Sun. There is no evidence that people can be infected by air conditioners in their cars or by window units in their homes.

Legionnaires' disease is a major bacterial disease that had existed without being detected until 1976. What made it suddenly known to science was the fact that so many people in the same place got sick all at once, attracting a lot of media attention and suggesting that something had infected them. What they had in common was the fact that they all had spent some time in the same convention hall. Remarkably, the CDC eventually found that these people were the victims of a fairly common, natural bacteria that has been invading humans and other hosts for centuries but of which no one had any knowledge.

[*See also* **Disease**]

Lens

Lenses are carefully shaped pieces of glass, plastic, or other transparent material. They are designed to manipulate light rays to create particular kinds of images. For example, the lenses in a telescope are designed to produce an enlarged view of a faraway object. Other common form of lenses are those found in eyeglasses, cameras, and microscopes.

Pioneers in lens development

Italian scientist Galileo Galilei (1564–1642) and Dutch scientist Antoni van Leeuwenhoek (1632–1723) were among the first to use lenses extensively in scientific research. Other scientists—French mathematician René Descartes (pronounced ren-AY day-KART; 1596–1650) and English scientist Isaac Newton (1642–1727), among others—dedicated most of their lives to improving lens designs. Despite the amount of time it has been in existence, the lens remains one of the simplest and most useful optical tools available.

Figure 1. (Reproduced by permission of The Gale Group.)

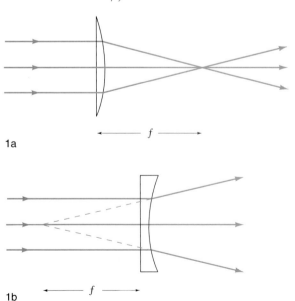

1a

1b

How lenses work

Lenses work on two principles: that light always travels in straight lines, and that it travels more slowly through glass or plastic than it does through air.

Light bends when it exits one substance (the air) and enters another (a lens). It bends again as it leaves the lens. The amount of bending depends greatly upon how much the lens is curved. All lenses have at least one curved surface, and most have two. There are two kinds of lenses, classified by how they are curved. Convex lenses (also called converging or positive) are thick in the middle and thin along the edges. Concave lenses (also called diverging or negative) are thin in the middle and thick along the edges. Each design bends and affects light differently.

Convex lenses

A convex lens bends light toward a central point (see Figure 1a). The farther from the center of the lens a beam of light strikes, the more the resulting light (f) is bent. Assuming an object is more than one focal length (a specific distance determined by the construction of the lens) away from the lens, the image viewed through a convex lens is always upside down. This is called a real image, and it can be projected upon a screen. The real image can be smaller or larger than the original object, also depending upon its distance from the lens.

Convex lenses magnify or enlarge objects. This type of lens is used in microscopes, telescopes, and binoculars.

Concave lenses

Concave lenses bend light away from a central axis (see Figure 1b). Similar to a convex lens, the light that strikes near the edge of the concave lens is bent more sharply away from the central axis (f). The image seen through a concave lens is called a virtual image. It is always right side up and cannot be projected. The virtual image is always smaller than the original, no matter what its distance from the lens.

Individual lenses cannot form sharp, flawless images over a wide field, and the images are always accompanied by distortion and color aberrations. Thus, most optical devices use systems of lenses that often assemble convex and concave lenses in precise combinations to minimize distortion or produce various effects.

Certain lenses, called plano-concave and plano-convex, are curved on only one side. Optical correction lenses, such as those used in eyeglasses, are ground with one side concave and one convex. Convexoconcave lenses aid patients who are nearsighted, while farsighted patients require concavo-convex lenses.

[*See also* **Telescope**]

Light

Light is generally defined as that portion of the electromagnetic spectrum with wavelengths between 400 and 700 nanometers (billionths of a

Words to Know

Corpuscle: A particle.

Diffraction: The bending of light or another form of electromagnetic radiation as it passes through a tiny hole or around a sharp edge.

Duality: The tendency of something to behave in two very different ways, for example, as both energy and matter.

Electromagnetic spectrum: The whole range of radiation that travels through a vacuum with a speed of about 3×10^8 meters per second.

Ether: Also spelled aether; medium that was hypothesized by physicists to explain the wave behavior of light.

Photoelectric effect: The production of an electric current when a beam of light is shined on a metal.

Photon: A tiny package of light energy.

Wave: A regular pattern of motion that involves some kind of disturbance in a medium.

Wavelength: The distance between two successive identical parts of a wave, such as two crests or two troughs.

meter). Like all forms of electromagnetic radiation, light travels with a speed of 186,282 miles (299,728 kilometers) per second in a vacuum. It is perhaps the swiftest and most delicate form of energy found in nature.

Historical concepts

Considering how important light is in our daily lives, it is hardly surprising that philosophers and scientists have been trying to understand its fundamental nature for centuries. The ancient Greeks, for example, worked out some of the basic laws involving light, including the laws of reflection (bouncing off an object) and refraction (bending through an object). They did so in spite of the fact that they started with only an incorrect concept of light. They believed that light beams started out in the human eye and traveled to an object.

With the rise of modern physics in the seventeenth century, scientists argued over two fundamental explanations of the nature of light: wave versus particle. According to the particle theory of light, light consists of a stream of particles that come from a source (such as the Sun or a lamp), travel to an object, and are then reflected to an observer. This view of light was first ˈproposed in some detail by Isaac Newton (1642–1727). Newton's theory is sometimes known as the corpuscular theory of light.

At about the same time, the wave theory of light was being developed. According to the wave theory, light travels through space in the form of a wave, similar in some ways to water waves. The primary spokesperson for this concept was Dutch physicist Christiaan Huygens (1629–1695).

Over time, the wave theory became more popular among physicists. One of the main reasons for the triumph of the wave theory was that many typical wave properties were detected for light. For example, when light passes through a tiny pinhole or around a sharp edge, it exhibits a property known as diffraction. Diffraction is well known as a property of waves among physicists. Almost anyone can witness the diffraction of water waves as they enter a bay or harbor, for example. If light exhibits diffraction, scientists thought, then it must be transmitted by waves.

Today, scientists usually talk about light as if it were transmitted by waves. They talk about the wavelength and frequency of light, both properties of waves, not particles.

The mysterious ether

One of the serious problems arising out of the wave theory of light is the problem of medium. Wave motion is the regular up-and-down motion of some material. For water waves, that material (or medium) is water. If light is a form of wave motion, scientists asked, what is the medium through which it travels?

The obvious answer, of course, is that light travels through air as a medium. But that answer is contradicted by the fact that light also travels through a vacuum, a region of space that contains no air or anything else.

To resolve this problem, scientists developed the concept of an ether (or aether). The ether was defined as a very thin material—perhaps like air, but much less dense—that permeates all of space. Light could be explained, then, as a wave motion in the ether.

Unfortunately, efforts to locate the ether were unsuccessful. In one of the most famous negative experiments of all time, two American physicists, Albert A. Michelson (1852–1931) and Edward W. Morley (1838–1923), devised a very precise method for detecting the ether. No matter how carefully they searched, they found no ether. Their experiments were so carefully designed and carried out that physicists were convinced that the ether did not exist.

Today, a somewhat simpler view of light as a wave phenomenon exists. Light is a form of radiation that needs no medium through which to travel. It consists of electric and magnetic fields that pulsate up and down as they travel through space.

Return of the corpuscular theory

By the early 1900s, most physicists had accepted the idea that light is a form of wave motion. But they did so somewhat reluctantly because some facts about light could not really be explained by the wave theory. The most important of these was the photoelectric effect.

The photoelectric effect was first observed by German physicist Heinrich Hertz (1857–1894) in about 1888. He noticed that when light is shined on a piece of metal, an electric current (a flow of electrons) is produced. Later experiments showed a rather peculiar property of the photoelectric effect. It doesn't make any difference how intense the light is that is shined on the metal. A bright light and a dim light both produce the same current. What does make a difference is the color of the light. Red light, for example, produces more of a current than blue light.

Unfortunately, there is no way for the wave theory of light to explain this effect. In fact, it was not until 1905 that a satisfactory explanation of the photoelectric effect was announced. That explanation came from German-born American physicist Albert Einstein (1879–1955). Einstein showed that the photoelectric effect could be explained provided that light were thought of not as a wave but as a bundle of tiny particles.

But the concept of light-as-particles is just what Isaac Newton had proposed more than 200 years earlier—and what physicists had largely rejected. The important point about Einstein's explanation, however, was that it worked. It explained a property of light that wave theory could not explain.

Duality of light and matter

The conflict between light-as-waves and light-as-particles has had an interesting resolution. Today, physicists say that light sometimes acts like a wave and sometimes acts like a collection of particles. Perhaps it is a wave consisting of tiny particles. Those particles are now called photons. They are different from other kinds of particles we know of since they have no mass. They are just tiny packages of energy that act like particles of matter.

Čerenkov Effect

The Čerenkov effect (pronounced che-REN-kof) is the emission of light from something transparent when a charged particle travels through the material with a speed faster than the speed of light in that material. The effect is named for Russian physicist Pavel A. Čerenkov (1904–1990), who first observed it in 1934.

Many people have seen the Čerenkov effect without realizing it. In photographs of a nuclear power plant, the water surrounding the reactor core often seems to glow with an eery blue light. That light is Čerenkov radiation produced when rapidly moving particles produced in the core travel through the cooling water around it.

The definition of the Čerenkov effect often puzzles students because it includes references to charged particles traveling faster than the speed of light. Of course, nothing can travel faster than the speed of light in a vacuum. In a fluid such as air, water, plastic, or glass, however, it is possible for objects to travel faster than the speed of light. When they do so, they produce the bluish glow seen in a nuclear reactor.

Two sets of laws are used to describe light. One set is based on the idea that light is a wave. Those laws are used when they work. The second set is based on the idea that light consists of particles. Those laws are also used when they work.

The philosophy of using wave or particle explanations for light is an example of duality. The term duality means that some natural phenomenon can be understood in two very different ways. Interestingly enough, other forms of duality have been discovered. For example, scientists have traditionally thought of electrons as a form of matter. They have mass and charge, which are characteristics of matter. But it happens that some properties of electrons can best be explained if they are thought of as waves. So, like light, electrons also have a dual character.

Making light stand still

In January 2001, scientists at two separate laboratories in Cambridge, Massachusetts, conducted landmark experiments in which they brought light particles to a halt and then sped them back up to their normal speed.

In the experiments, the scientists created chambers that held a gas. One research team used sodium gas, the other used the gas form of rubidium, an alkaline metal element. The gases in both chambers were chilled magnetically to within a few millionths of a degree of absolute zero, or $-459°F$ ($-273°C$). The scientists passed a light beam into the specially prepared chambers, and the light became fainter and fainter as it slowed and then eventually stopped. Even thought the light vanished, the information on its particles was still imprinted on the atoms of sodium and rubidium. That information was basically frozen or stored. The scientists then flashed a second light through the gas, which essentially reconstituted or revived the original beam. The light left each of the chambers with almost the same shape, intensity, and other properties it had when it entered the chambers.

Scientists believe the biggest impact of these experiments could come in futuristic technologies such as ultra-fast quantum computers. The light could be made to carry so-called quantum information, which involves particles that can exist in many places or states at once. Computers employing such technology could run through operations vastly faster than existing machines.

[*See also* **Electromagnetic spectrum; Interference; Photoelectric effect; Wave motion**]

Light-year

The speed of light is one of the most fundamental measurements in astronomy. Measured in miles or kilometers per second, the speed of light determines distance. The term light-year refers to the distance light travels in a vacuum in one year. Since light travels at slightly more than 186,000 miles (300,000 kilometers) per second, one light-year is roughly equal to 5.9 trillion miles (9.5 trillion kilometers).

The light-year is a convenient unit of measurement to use when discussing distances to the stars in the Milky Way galaxy and throughout the observable universe. When considering distances within our solar system, the astronomical unit (AU) is commonly used. One AU—the mean distance between Earth and the Sun—is roughly equal to 93 million miles (150 million kilometers). One light-year equals about 63,500 astronomical units.

The sky is a map of celestial history. The light from the Sun takes just over eight minutes to reach Earth. When we look at the Sun, we don't see how the Sun appears, but how it appeared eight minutes ago. If you look at something in the sky that is eight light-years away, you are seeing light that left that object eight years ago. You are therefore looking backward in time, seeing that object in the condition it was eight years ago. In this sense, a light-year can also be thought of as a measurement of time.

Alpha Centauri, the closest star to Earth, is 4.35 light-years distant. The center of the Milky Way galaxy is 27,000 light-years away, while the most distant clusters of galaxies are roughly estimated to be one million light-years away.

Lipids

The lipids are a class of biochemical compounds, many of which occur naturally in plants and animals. (Biochemical compounds are organic compounds that are intimately involved in living organisms.) Most organic compounds are classified into one of a few dozen families, based on their structural similarities. The lipids are an exception to that rule. The members of this family are classified together because they all have a single common physical property: they do not dissolve in water, but they do dissolve in organic solvents such as alcohols, ethers, benzene, chloroform, and carbon tetrachloride.

The lipids constitute a very large class of compounds, many of which play essential roles in organisms. Among the most important lipids are fats and oils, waxes, steroids, terpenes, fat-soluble vitamins, prostaglandins, phosphoglycerides, sphingolipids, and glycolipids. Some of these names may be unfamiliar to the general reader, but they all are vital to the growth and development of plants and animals. Phospholipids, for example, occur in all living organisms, where they are a major component of the membranes of most cells. They are especially abundant in liver, brain, and spinal tissue.

Waxes, fats, and oils

Perhaps the most common and most familiar examples of the lipids are the waxes, fats, and oils. All three classes of compounds have somewhat similar structures. They are made by the reaction between an alcohol and a fatty acid. (A fatty acid is an organic compound that consists of a very long chain of carbon atoms with a characteristic acid group at one end of the chain.) Fats and oils differ from waxes because of the chemical composition of the alcohols from which they are made. Fats and oils differ from each other in one major way: fats are solids; oils are liquid. These differences in physical state reflect differences in the kinds of fatty acids from which these two types of compounds are made.

Fats in animal bodies

Fats are an important part of animal bodies, where they have four main functions. First, they are a source of energy. Although carbohydrates are often regarded as the primary source of energy in an organism, fats actually provide more than twice as much energy per calorie as do carbohydrates.

Fats also provide insulation for the body, protecting against excessive heat losses to the environment. Third, fats act as a protective cushion around bones and organs. Finally, fats store certain vitamins, such as vitamins A, D, E, and K, that are not soluble in water but are soluble in fats and oils.

Animal bodies are able to synthesize (produce) the fats they need from the foods that make up their diets. Among humans, 25 to 50 percent of the typical diet may consist of fats and oils. In general, a healthful diet is thought to be one that contains a smaller, rather than larger, proportion of fats.

The main use of fats commercially is in the production of soaps and other cleaning products. When a fat is boiled in water in the presence of a base such as sodium hydroxide, the fat breaks down into compounds known as glycerol and fatty acids. The fatty acids formed in this reaction react with sodium hydroxide to produce a soap. The process of making soap from a fatty material is known as saponification.

[*See also* **Metabolism; Organic chemistry**]

Lock

A lock or water lock is an enclosed, rectangular chamber with gates at each end, within which water is raised or lowered to allow boats or ships to overcome differences in water level. Locks have a history of over 2,000 years, and although they are most often used by boats on canals, they also are used to transport massive ships between seas.

All locks operate on the simple buoyancy principle that any vessel, no matter what size, will float atop a large enough volume of water. By raising or lowering the level of a body of water, the vessel itself goes up or down accordingly. Locks are used to connect two bodies of water that are at different ground levels as well as to "walk" a vessel up or down a river's more turbulent parts. This is done by a series of connecting or "staircase" locks. Locks contributed significantly to the Industrial Revolution (period beginning about the middle of the eighteenth century during which humans began to use steam engines as a major source of power) by making possible the interconnection of canals and rivers, thus broadening commerce. They still play a major role in today's industrial society.

History

The ancestor of the modern lock is the flash lock. It originated in China and is believed to have been used as early as 50 B.C. The flash lock was a navigable gap in a masonry dam that could be opened or closed by a single wooden gate. Opening the gate very quickly would release a sudden surge of water that was supposed to assist a vessel downstream through shallow water. This was often very dangerous. Using the flash lock to go upstream was usually safe but extremely slow since the gap in the dam was used to winch or drag a vessel through.

At some future date, a second gate was added to the flash lock, thus giving birth to the pound lock. The first known example of a pound lock (whose dual gates "impound" or capture the water) was in China in A.D. 984. It consisted of two flash locks about 250 feet (76 meters) apart. By raising or lowering guillotine or up-and-down gates at each end, water was captured or released. The space between the two gates thus acted as an equalizing chamber that elevated or lowered a vessel to meet the next water level. This new method was entirely controllable and had none of the hazards and surges of the old flash lock.

Ships in the Miraflores locks on the Panama Canal. *(Reproduced by permission of Photo Researchers, Inc.)*

The first pound lock in Europe was built at Vreeswijk, the Netherlands, in 1373. Like its Chinese ancestor, it also had guillotine gates. The pound lock system spread quickly throughout Europe during the next century, but was eventually replaced by an improved system that formed the basis of the modern lock system. During the fifteenth century, Italian artist and scientist Leonardo da Vinci (1452–1519) devised an improved form of pound lock whose gates formed a V-shape when closed. In 1487, Leonardo built six locks with gates of this type. These gates turned on hinges, like doors, and when closed they formed a V-shape pointing upstream—thus giving them their name of miter gates. One great advantage of miter gates was that they were self-sealing from the pressure of the upsteam water.

Construction and operation

The earliest locks were built entirely of wood, with stone and then brick becoming standard materials. The gates themselves were always wooden, with some lasting as long as 50 years. Filling or emptying these early locks was often accomplished by hand-operated sluices or floodgates built in the gates. On later and larger locks, it was found that conduits or culverts built into the lock wall itself were not only more efficient but let the water enter in a smoother, more controlled manner. Nearly all locks operate in the following manner: (1) A vessel going downstream to shallower water enters a lock with the front gate closed. (2) The rear gate is then closed and the water level in the lock is lowered by opening a valve. The vessel goes down as the water escapes. (3) When the water level inside the lock is as low as that downstream, the front gate is opened and the vessel continues on its way. To go upstream, the process is reversed, with the water level being raised inside the lock. What the operators always strive for is to fill or empty the lock in the fastest time possible with a minimum of turbulence.

In modern locks, concrete and steel have replaced wood and brick, and hydraulic power or electricity is used to open and close the gates and side sluices. Movable gates are the most important part of a lock, and they must be strong enough to withstand the water pressure arising from the often great difference in water levels. They are mostly a variation of Leonardo's miter gates, except now they usually are designed to be stored inside the lock's wall recesses.

Probably the best known locks in the world are those used in the Panama Canal—the most-used canal in the world. Completed in 1914, the Panama Canal is an interoceanic waterway 51 miles (82 kilometers) long that connects the Atlantic and Pacific Oceans through the Isthmus of Panama. It has three major sets of locks, each of which is built in tandem to allow vessels to move in either direction, like a separated, two-way street. Each lock gate has two leaves, 65 feet (20 meters) wide by 7 feet (2 meter) thick, set on hinges. The gates range in height from 47 to 82 feet (14 to 25 meters) and are powered by large motors built in the lock walls. The chambers are 1,000 feet (305 meters) long, 110 feet (34 meters) wide, and 41 feet (13 meters) deep. Most large vessels are towed through the locks. As with all locks today, they are operated from a control tower using visual signals and radio communications.

[*See also* **Canal**]

Logarithm

In the 1500s and early 1600s, although science, engineering, and medicine were flourishing, many people did not understand multiplication tables. Mathematicians, astronomers, navigators, and scientists were forced to spend a lot of time performing calculations, so that little time was left to work on experiments and new discoveries. Finally, around 1594 Scottish mathematician John Napier (1550–1617) produced a table of logarithmic, or proportionate, numbers.

How logarithms work

In the commonly known base 10 system, computations that involve very large numbers can become difficult, if not incomprehensible. Napier realized numbers could be more easily expressed in terms of powers. Thus 100 is equal to 10 multiplied by 10, written as 10^2. This is read as "10 squared" and means "10 to the power two."

To perform multiplication, numbers are converted into logarithms, the exponents added together, and the result converted back into base 10. Likewise, to perform division, two logarithmic exponents are subtracted, and the result converted back to base 10.

This innovative way of multiplying and dividing large numbers was a milestone event for mathematicians of the day. Napier's tables were published in 1614 and were put into use immediately, becoming an essential part of the mathematical, scientific, and navigational processes.

Logarithmic tables remained popular throughout the next several centuries and were used as the basis for many mechanical calculating devices. Relieved from much of their mental drudgery, scientists and mathematicians enjoyed new freedom in their work, allowing them to focus their attention on new scientific breakthroughs.

Luminescence

The term luminescence is used to describe a process by which light is produced other than by heating. The production of light from heat, or incandescence, is familiar to everyone. The Sun gives off both heat and light as a result of nuclear reactions in its core. An incandescent lightbulb gives off light when a wire filament inside the bulb is heated to white heat. One can read by the light of a candle flame because burning wax gives off both heat and light.

But light can also be produced by other processes in which heat is not involved. For example, fireflies produce light by means of chemical reactions that take place within their bodies. They convert a compound known as luciferin from one form into another. As that process occurs, light is given off.

Fireflies have a bioluminescent organ in their abdomen that they use to attract mates. Chemicals within the organ react with oxygen to produce light. The insect controls the flashes by regulating the flow of oxygen. (*Reproduced by permission of The Stock Market.*)

▼ Words to Know

Fluorescence: Luminescence that stops within 10 nanoseconds after an energy source has been removed.

Incandescence: Light created by heating. Incandescence is not a luminescent process.

Phosphor: A material that absorbs energy over some period of time, then gives off light for a longer period.

Phosphorescence: Luminescence that continues for more than 10 nanoseconds after an energy source has been removed.

Fluorescence and phosphorescence

Two forms of luminescence can be identified, depending on the amount of time emitted light continues to glow. By definition, fluorescence refers to the release of light that lasts no more than about 10 nanoseconds (10 billionths of a second) after it begins. Phosphorescence refers to the release of light that lasts longer than 10 nanoseconds.

Substances that glow in the dark have many practical applications today. Clocks and watches, for example, often have their numbers and hands coated with phosphorescent paints so we can see what time it is in the dark. Emergency doors and stairways are also highlighted with these paints so that people can find their way out in case of a power failure.

Probably the most familiar form of fluorescence is a fluorescent lightbulb. Fluorescent light is produced when an electrical current passes through mercury vapor in the lightbulb. Electrons produced from the mercury vapor collide with a chemical painted on the inside of the bulb, causing fluorescence. The moment the bulb is turned off, however, the chemical stops glowing. The light produced by this process, therefore, is an example of fluorescence.

Many people have seen minerals that are phosphorescent. Once exposed to light, they continue to glow for many minutes after being placed into a dark room. The longer glow time defines these minerals as phosphorescent.

Processes that create luminescence

The changes that take place in atoms during luminescence are the same as those that occur during incandescence. Electrons in atoms absorb energy from some source and jump to a higher energy level. After a fraction of a second, the electrons fall back to their original level, giving off the energy they had previously absorbed.

Various procedures can be used to get this process started, that is, to get electrons to jump to higher energy levels. In incandescence, the process is heating. In luminescence, it can be any one of a number of other processes.

In chemiluminescence, for example, some chemical reaction occurs that gives off energy. That energy is then used to excite electrons and produce luminescence. Many students are familiar with devices called cyalume sticks. When one of these sticks is broken, two chemicals are released and begin to react with each other. The energy released during that reaction produces luminescence that can last for many hours.

Bioluminescence is a kind of chemiluminescence in which the chemical reaction involved takes place within a living organism. The example of light production by fireflies is an example of bioluminescence.

Electroluminescence occurs when an electric current passes through a material, causing the material to glow. Many flat-panel displays on electronic equipment, such as those on laptop computers, contain electroluminescent systems.

Less common examples of luminescence are those produced by sound energy (sonoluminescence) and by friction (triboluminescence).

Lymphatic system

The lymphatic system is a network of vessels that transports nutrients to the cells and collects their waste products. The lymph system consists of lymph capillaries and lymph vessels that are somewhat similar to blood capillaries and blood vessels. In addition, it includes lymph ducts (tubes that carry fluids secreted by glands) and lymph nodes (reservoirs that filter out bacteria and other toxins from the lymph that passes through them).

In the circulatory system, blood flows from the heart, through the arteries, and into capillaries that surround all cells. When blood reaches the capillaries, a portion of blood plasma (the liquid portion of the blood)

⍒ Words to Know

Capillaries: Tiny vessels in the body that carry fluids such as lymph and blood.

Lymph: A fluid that runs through the lymphatic vessels, lymph nodes, and other lymphatic organs.

Lymphocyte: A cell that functions as part of the lymphatic and immune systems by attacking specific invading substances.

Lymph node: Region of lymphoid tissue along lymph vessels that filters harmful antigens from the blood and some tissues.

Osmosis: Process in which fluids and substances dissolved in liquids pass through a membrane until all substances involved reach a balance.

seeps out of the capillaries and into the space surrounding cells. That plasma is then known as tissue fluid. Tissue fluid consists of water plus dissolved molecules that are small enough to fit through the small openings in capillaries.

Tissue fluid is an important component of any living animal. Nutrients pass out of tissue fluid into cells and, conversely, waste products from cells are dumped back into the tissue fluid.

Some tissue fluid returns to blood capillaries by osmosis. (Osmosis is the process by which fluids and substances dissolved in them pass through a membrane until all substances involved reach a balance.) But some tissue fluid is also diverted into a second network of tubes: the lymphatic vessels. Tissue fluid that enters this network is known as lymph. Lymph is a clear, colorless, somewhat sticky liquid. The liquid formed in a blister is lymph.

Movement of lymph

Tissue fluid passes out of the space between cells and through the walls of lymph capillaries. Now called lymph, it follows a pathway back to the heart that is somewhat similar to the venous system for blood. It passes from lymph capillaries into larger tubes, the lymph vessels. Like veins in the blood circulatory system, lymph vessels have valves that help push lymph slowly back towards the heart. Eventually the lymph enters a large collecting tube, the thoracic duct, located near the heart. From the thoracic duct the lymph empties into the blood circulatory system itself at the left subclavian vein.

The lymph system performs a second function also. Fats that have been absorbed in the small intestine enter lymph vessels in that organ. Those fats are then carried through the lymphatic system back into the blood circulatory system.

Lymph nodes

At various points in the lymphatic system the lymphatic vessels are enlarged to form structures known as lymph nodes. Lymph nodes serve four primary functions. First, they remove from the lymph foreign particles dumped into the tissue fluid from cells. Second, they produce a type of white blood cell known as lymphocytes. Lymphocytes are major components of the body's immune system, which fights disease. They occur

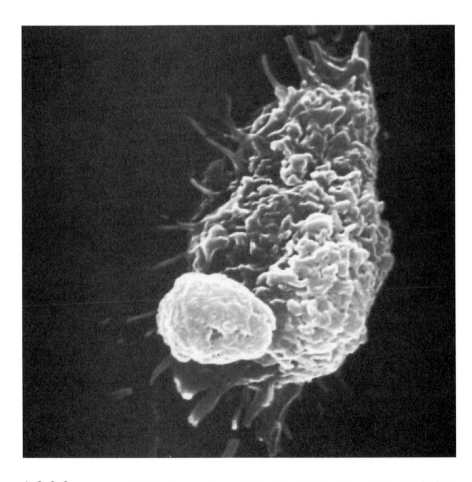

A macrophage (background) and a lymphocyte (foreground). *(Reproduced by permission of Phototake.)*

in a variety of forms known as T cells (T lymphocytes) and B cells (B lymphocytes). Third, lymph nodes are home to very large blood cells known as macrophages. Macrophages attack and kill bacteria by surrounding them, swallowing them up, and then dissolving them with enzymes. Fourth, lymph nodes produce antibodies that are used to fight infections.

Lymph nodes are located in the armpit, neck, and groin. One symptom of an infection is that lymph nodes become swollen with harmful material and can be seen or felt.

Diseases of the lymphatic system

The uncontrolled growth of cells and tissues of the lymphatic system result in a condition known as lymphoma, or lymph cancer. Lymphomas are classified into two types, Hodgkin's or non-Hodgkin's. Both forms can be fatal. Hodgkin's lymphoma, or Hodgkin's disease, is marked by enlargement of lymph nodes, usually those in the neck. Symptoms of Hodgkin's include chronic fatigue, depressed immune function, weight loss, night sweats, and pain after drinking alcohol. Hodgkin's lymphoma can be treated successfully and cured with radiation or chemotherapy if it is caught in its early stages. Although the cause of Hodgkin's is unknown, males, Caucasians, people of higher socioeconomic status, the well-educated, and people with certain blood types are more prone to develop it. For unknown reasons, Hodgkin's most commonly affects people in their twenties or seventies. People who work with certain chemicals, such as benzene and rubber products, also seem to be more prone to develop the disease.

Several forms of non-Hodgkin's lymphoma have been identified. These forms have little in common with each other. One example of a non-Hodgkin's lymphoma is Burkitt's lymphoma, prevalent among Central African children. Burkitt's lymphoma is characterized by enlargement of the lymph nodes under the jaw. In contrast with most lymphomas whose causes are unclear, Burkitt's lymphoma has been linked to infection with the Epstein-Barr virus.

Symptoms for most lymphomas are similar. Many patients experience enlargement of the liver and spleen as well as the lymph nodes. Some patients have bloody stools or vomit blood. Tiredness, itching, weight loss, fever, and general failure of the immune system may also be present. These symptoms may diminish and intensify over several months before a diagnosis is made. Sometimes, a bone marrow biopsy (test) is also performed.

Treatment includes radiation or chemotherapy. Effectiveness of such treatments varies depending on the severity of the lymphoma at the time of diagnosis. Bone marrow transplants have been effective against some lymphomas in advanced stages. The cure rate for non-Hodgkin's lymphomas is generally poorer than for Hodgkin's lymphomas.

[*See also* **Antibody and antigen; Immune system; Infection**]

Machines, simple

A simple machine is a device for doing work that has only one part. Simple machines redirect or change the size of forces, allowing people to do work with less muscle effort and greater speed, thus making their work easier. There are six kinds of simple machines: the lever, the pulley, the wheel and axle, the inclined plane, the wedge, and the screw.

Everyday work

We all do work in our daily lives and we all use simple machines every day. Work as defined by science is force acting upon an object in order to move it across a distance. So scientifically, whenever we push, pull, or cause something to move by using a force, we are performing work. A machine is basically a tool used to make this work easier, and a simple machine is among the simplest tools we can use. Therefore, from a scientific standpoint, we are doing work when we open a can of paint with a screwdriver, use a spade to pull out weeds, slide boxes down a ramp, or go up and down on a see-saw. In each of these examples we are using a simple machine that allows us to achieve our goal with less muscle effort or in a shorter amount of time.

Earliest simple machines

This idea of doing something in a better or easier way or of using less of our own muscle power has always been a goal of humans. Probably from the beginning of human history, anyone who ever had a job to do would eventually look for a way to do it better, quicker, and easier. Most people

▼ Words to Know

Compound machine: A machine consisting of two or more simple machines.

Effort force: The force applied to a machine.

Fulcrum: The point or support on which a lever turns.

Resistance force: The force exerted by a machine.

Work: Transfer of energy by a force acting to move matter.

try to make a physical job easier rather than harder to do. In fact, one of our human predecessors is called *Homo habilis,* which means "handy man" or "capable man." This early version of our human ancestors was given that name because, although not quite fully human, it had a large enough brain to understand the idea of a tool, as well as hands with fingers and thumbs that were capable of making and using a tool. Therefore, the first simple machine was probably a strong stick (the lever) that our ancestor used to move a heavy object, or perhaps it was a sharp rock (the wedge) used to scrape an animal skin, or something else equally simple but effective. Other early examples might be a rolling log, which is a primitive form of the wheel and axle, and a sloping hill, which is a natural inclined plane. There is evidence throughout all early civilizations that humans used simple machines to satisfy their needs and to modify their environment.

The beauty of simple machines is seen in the way they are used as extensions of our own muscles, as well as in how they can redirect or magnify the strength and force of an individual. They do this by increasing the efficiency of our work, as well as by what is called a mechanical advantage. A mechanical advantage occurs when a simple machine takes a small "input" force (our own muscle power) and increases the magnitude of the "output" force. A good example of this is when a person uses a small input force on a jack handle and produces an output force large enough to easily lift one end of an automobile. The efficiency and advantage produced by such a simple device can be amazing, and it was with such simple machines that the rock statues of Easter Island, the stone pillars of Stonehenge, and the Great Pyramids of Egypt were constructed. Some of the known accomplishments of these early users of simple machines are truly amazing. For example, we have evidence that the builders of the pyramids moved limestone blocks weighing between 2 and 70 tons (1.8 and 63.5 metric tons) hundreds of miles, and that they built ramps over 1 mile (1.6 kilometers) long.

Trade-offs of simple machines

One of the keys to understanding how a simple machine makes things easier is to realize that the amount of work a machine can do is equal to the force used, multiplied by the distance that the machine moves or lifts the object. In other words, we can multiply the force we are able to exert if we increase the distance. For example, the longer the inclined plane—which is basically a ramp—the smaller the force needed to move an object. Picture having to lift a heavy box straight up off the ground and place it on a high self. If the box is too heavy for us to pick up, we can build a ramp (an inclined plane) and push it up. Common sense tells us that the steeper (or shorter) the ramp, the harder it is to push the object to the top. Yet the longer (and less steep) it is, the easier it is to move the box, little by little. Therefore, if we are not in a hurry (like the pyramid builders), we can take our time and push it slowly up the long ramp to the top of the shelf.

Understanding this allows us also to understand that simple machines involve what is called a "trade-off." The trade-off, or the something that is given up in order to get something else, is the increase in distance. So although we have to use less force to move a heavy object up a ramp, we have increased the distance we have to move it (because a ramp is not the shortest distance between two points). Most primitive people were happy to make this trade-off since it often meant being able to move something that they otherwise could not have moved.

Today, most machines are complicated and use several different elements like ball bearings or gears to do their work. However, when we look at them closely and understand their parts, we usually see that despite their complexity they are basically just two or more simple machines working together. These are called compound machines. Although some people say that there are less than six simple machines (since a wedge can be considered an inclined plane that is moving, or a pulley is a lever that rotates around a fixed point), most authorities agree that there are in fact six types of simple machines.

Lever

A lever is a stiff bar or rod that rests on a support called a fulcrum (pronounced FULL-krum) and which lifts or moves something. This may be one of the earliest simple machines, because any large, strong stick would have worked as a lever. Pick up a stick, wedge it under one edge of a rock, and push down and you have used a lever. Downward motion on one end results in upward motion on the other. Anything that pries something loose is also a lever, such as a crow bar or the claw end of a hammer. There are three types or classes of levers. A first-class lever has the fulcrum or pivot point located near the middle of the tool and what it is moving (called the resistance force). A pair of scissors and a seesaw are good examples. A second-class lever has the resistance force located between the fulcrum and the end of the lever where the effort force is being made. Typical examples of this are a wheelbarrow, nutcracker, and a bottle opener. A third-class lever has the effort force being applied between the fulcrum and the resistance force. Tweezers, ice tongs, and shovels are good examples. When you use a shovel, you hold one end steady to act as a fulcrum, and you use your other hand to pull up on a load of dirt. The second hand is the effort force, and the dirt being picked up is

This man is demonstrating the use of a lever (the board) and fulcrum. (Reproduced by permission of Photo Researchers, Inc.)

the resistance force. The effort applied by your second hand lies between the resistance force (dirt) and the fulcrum (your first hand).

Pulley

A pulley consists of a grooved wheel that turns freely in a frame called a block through which a rope runs. In some ways, it is a variation of a wheel and axle, but instead of rotating an axle, the wheel rotates a rope or cord. In its simplest form, a pulley's grooved wheel is attached to some immovable object, like a ceiling or a beam. When a person pulls down on one end of the rope, an object at the opposite end is raised. A simple pulley gains nothing in force, speed, or distance. Instead, it only changes the direction of the force, as with a Venetian blind (up or down). Pulley systems can be movable and very complex, using two or more connected pulleys. This permits a heavy load to be lifted with less force, although over a longer distance.

Wheel and axle

The wheel and axle is actually a variation of the lever (since the center of the axle acts as the fulcrum). It may have been used as early as 3000 B.C., and like the lever, it is a very important simple machine. However, unlike the lever that can be rotated to pry an object loose or push a load along, a wheel and axle can move a load much farther. Since it consists of a large wheel rigidly attached to a small wheel (the axle or the shaft), when one part turns the other also does. Some examples of the wheel and axle are a door knob, a water wheel, an egg beater, and the wheels on a wagon, car, or bicycle. When force is applied to the wheel (thereby turning the axle), force is increased and distance and speed are decreased. When it is applied to the axle (turning the wheel), force is decreased and distance and speed are increased.

Inclined plane

An inclined plane is simply a sloping surface. It is used to make it easier to move a weight from a lower to a higher spot. It takes much less effort to push a wheel barrow load slowly up a gently sloping ramp than it does to pick it up and lift it to a higher spot. The trade-off is that the load must be moved a greater distance. Everyday examples are stairs, escalators, ladders, and a ship's plank.

Wedge

A wedge is an inclined plane that moves and is used to increase force—either to separate something or to hold things together. With a wedge, the object or material remains in place while the wedge moves. A wedge can have a single sloping surface (like a door stop that holds a door tightly in place), or it can have two sloping surfaces or sides (like the wedge that splits a log in two). An axe or knife blade is a wedge, as is a chisel, plow, and even a nail.

Screw

A screw can be considered yet another form of an inclined plane, since it can be thought of as one that is wrapped in a spiral around a cylinder or post. In everyday life, screws are used to hold things together and to lift other things. When it is turned, a screw converts rotary (circular) motion into a forward or backward motion. Every screw has two parts: a body or post around which the inclined plane is twisted, and the thread (the spiraled inclined plane itself). Every screw has a thread, and if you look very closely at it, you will see that the threads form a tiny "ramp"

The gears that power a film projector. *(Reproduced by permission of Thomas Video.)*

that runs from the tip to the top. Like nails, screws are used to hold things together, while a drill bit is used to make holes. Other examples of screws are airplane and boat propellers.

Magnetic recording/ audiocassette

Audiocassette tape recorders are widely used to record and play back music or speech. Information is stored on a narrow ribbon of plastic tape that has one side coated with a magnetic material consisting of magnetically active particles, most commonly iron oxide and chromium dioxide. As the tape passes around the five magnetic heads of a tape recorder, sound is recorded, replayed, or erased according to the heads that are activated.

A recording head (a small electromagnet) magnetizes the passing tape in such a way that the magnetic particles on it are realigned in a pattern that corresponds to the loudness and frequency (rate of vibration) of

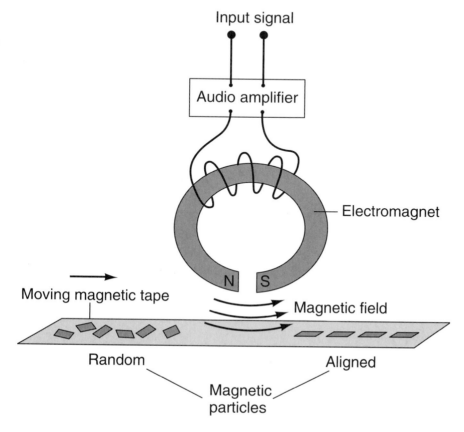

Recording head.
(Reproduced by permission of The Gale Group.)

Words to Know

Digital audio tape (DAT): A technology developed in the 1990s, by which information is stored on magnetic tape in binary code.

Electromagnet: A coil of wire surrounding an iron core that becomes magnetized when electric current flows through the wire.

Erase head: An electromagnet operating at an ultrasonic frequency (rate of vibration) to scramble previously recorded information on a tape.

Playback head: A small coil that senses the varying magnetic field of the moving tape and converts it into an electrical signal that can be amplified.

Recording head: An electromagnet that aligns the magnetic particles of the cassette tape while it moves by.

incoming sounds. The resulting pattern remains on the tape until erased or changed.

The tape of an audiocassette has a weak magnetic field (an area where a magnetic force is present) around it that varies from point to point depending on the pattern of its magnetic particles. The playback head contains a coil of wire. When the magnetized tape moves past the coil, an electrical current is created. The current will alternate in direction depending on the alignment of the magnetic particles as they pass by the playback head. The magnetic pattern originally recorded on the tape is transformed into a precisely corresponding electrical signal.

The electric current from the playback head is then amplified and sent to an audio speaker, which vibrates simultaneously with the varying current. The back-and-forth motion of the speaker creates pressure waves in the air. This causes the listener's eardrums to vibrate, producing the sensation of sound.

An audiocassette has a built-in erase head to remove previously recorded information. The tape has to be blank before it can be used again to make a new recording. The erase head normally is an electromagnet that operates at an ultrasonic frequency, much higher than the human ear can hear. It effectively scrambles the previously recorded magnetic particle patterns. Audiocassettes are designed so that the tape from the supply reel passes by the erase head just before the recording head.

History of magnetic recording

The invention of magnetic recording tape is attributed to both American inventor J. A. O'Neill and German engineer Fritz Pfleumer (1881–1945). Pfleumer filed the first audiotape patent in 1929. In 1935, the German electronics firm AEG produced a prototype (first version) of a record/playback machine, called a magnetophon. It was based on Pfleumer's idea, but used a plastic tape. Another firm, BASF, went on to refine the tape AEG used, presenting the first usable magnetic tape in 1935.

Types of magnetic recording machines

At one time, audiotape was used in a reel-to-reel format. This was a complicated and awkward procedure. Eight-track cartridges were another innovation in magnetic recording. These used an endless-loop format so the tape could be played continuously without being flipped over by the listener.

The audiocassette was introduced in 1963 by the Philips Company of the Netherlands. The audiocassette made inserting, advancing, and rewinding a tape fast and easy. The tape could be stopped and ejected at any point. Because of this ease and economy, magnetic tape recordings could compete with long-playing records (LPs). The invention of the microchip allowed audiotape players to be made smaller and more portable. With the introduction of products such as Sony's compact Walkman™, cassettes became universally popular.

Although the audiocassette is economical and still widely used, digital technologies are revolutionizing the industry. Digital audio tape

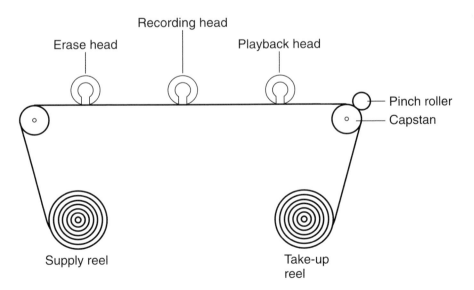

Cassette and heads. *(Reproduced by permission of The Gale Group.)*

(DAT) recorders became widely available in the United States in 1990. A digital system enables a home recorder to make a tape copy that is an exact replica (not just an approximation) of the original sounds on a cassette that is half the size of a typical audiocassette. Digital technology records sound in a code of binary numbers (a series of zeroes and ones), so each subsequent recording is an exact copy of the code. These kinds of recordings do not suffer from the sound distortion that was the problem with the recordings they replaced.

[*See also* **Electromagnetic field**]

Magnetism

Magnetism is a fundamental force of nature manifested by the attraction of certain materials for iron. Materials so attracted are said to be magnetic materials.

Humans have known about magnetism since at least 600 B.C. The force was almost certainly first observed in the attraction between the mineral known as lodestone, a form of magnetite, and pieces of iron. Englishman William Gilbert (1540–1603) was the first person to investigate the phenomenon of magnetism systematically using scientific methods. He also discovered that Earth is itself a weak magnet. Early theoretical investigations into the nature of Earth's magnetism were carried out by German physicist Carl Friedrich Gauss (1777–1855).

Some of the earliest quantitative studies of magnetic phenomena were initiated in the eighteenth century by French physicist Charles Coulomb (1736–1806). Coulomb found that the force between two magnetized objects is an inverse square law. That is, the force increases according to the magnetic strength of the two objects and decreases according to the square of the distance between them.

Danish physicist Hans Christian Oersted (1777–1851) first suggested a link between electricity and magnetism. Oersted found that an electric current always produces a magnetic field around itself. (A magnetic field is an area where a magnetic force is present.) Shortly thereafter, French physicist André-Marie Ampère (1775–1836) and English chemist and physicist Michael Faraday (1791–1869) demonstrated the opposite effect, namely that moving a wire through a magnetic field could produce an electric current in the wire.

The experimental work of Oersted, Ampère, Faraday, and others was brought together in a brilliant theoretical work by Scottish physicist James

Clerk Maxwell (1831–1879). Maxwell demonstrated that electricity and magnetism represent different aspects of the same fundamental force field.

Earth's magnetism

The magnetic force present in an object seems to be located in two distinct regions of the objects known as poles. One pole is known as the north magnetic pole, while the other is known as the south magnetic pole. The magnetic force appears to flow out of one pole and into the other pole. The region of space through which the magnetic force flows is called the magnetic field.

Earth itself acts like a giant magnet. One pole of Earth's magnet is close to the north geographic pole, and the other pole is close to the south geographic pole. The magnetic properties of Earth are thought to be due to the presence of a very large mass of iron located at the center of the planet. As that core rotates, it may generate the magnetic field that we can detect with a compass.

Nature of magnetism

The magnetic field is invisible. It can be detected, however, by spreading finely divided pieces of iron in the region around a magnet. In that case, the iron pieces arrange themselves in a pattern similar to that shown in the accompanying photograph. The white streaks in the photograph are known as magnetic lines of force, or flux lines. They indicate the regions in which the magnetic force appears to be strongest.

The laws describing magnetic poles are similar to those describing electrical forces. That is, like poles repel each other, and unlike poles attract each other. If two magnets are lined up with their south poles adjacent to (next to) each other, they will tend to push apart. If they are lined up with a north pole next to a south pole, they tend to draw close to each other. If an unmagnetized piece of iron is placed near either a north or a south pole, it is attracted to that pole.

Types of magnets

Two kinds of magnets exist: natural magnets and electromagnets. Magnetite and lodestone are two examples of natural magnets that occur in Earth. Any iron bar can also be made magnetic simply by rubbing it with magnetite, lodestone, or any other magnetic material. Bar magnets and horseshoe magnets are made in this way.

A second kind of magnet is an electromagnet. The magnetic field of an electromagnet is produced by wrapping an electric wire around a piece of iron. When an electric current flows through the wire, it creates a magnetic field in the iron. The strength of the magnetic field depends primarily on two factors: the number of turns of wire on the iron and the strength of the electric current.

The most powerful electromagnets known are made of superconducting materials. A superconducting material is one that carries an electric current without any resistance. Once an electric current is started in a superconducting material, it continues to travel through the material—essentially forever.

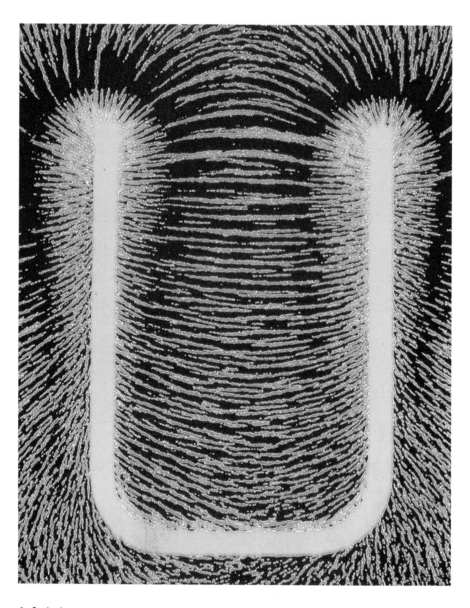

A computer graphic of a horseshoe magnet with iron filings aligned around it. *(Reproduced by permission of Photo Researchers, Inc.)*

The magnetic field surrounding a natural magnet, such as a bar or horseshoe magnet, measures a few hundred gauss. The gauss is one of the units used to measure the strength of a magnetic field. The magnetic field produced by an electromagnet, by contrast, is in the range of a few tens of thousands of gauss. The highest magnetic field achieved by a superconducting electromagnetic approaches 100,000 gauss in strength.

Origin of magnetism

Magnetism is caused by the motion of electrons in an atom. Picture an atom, consisting of a central core, the nucleus, and one or more electrons traveling around that core. Those electrons exhibit two kinds of motion. First, they travel around the nucleus of the atom in a manner somewhat similar to the motion of planets around the Sun. Second, they spin on their own axes, much as planets spin on their own axes.

Now recall how an electric current flowing through a wire sets up a magnetic field around that wire. In much the same way, a moving electron sets up a magnetic field around itself. Both the orbiting motion of the electron around the nucleus and the electron spin create magnetic fields.

In a magnetic material, atoms group themselves into microscopic regions called domains. All of the atoms within any given domain are aligned in the same direction. The domain itself, therefore, acts like a very tiny magnet with a south pole and a north pole.

Under most circumstances, however, the domains in a magnetic material are arranged in random order. They point in every which direction and, overall, cancel each other out. The material itself is not magnetic.

When the material is stroked with a magnet, however, the domains all line themselves up according to the magnetic field of the magnet. All the north poles of the tiny domain magnets are pulled in one direction, and the south poles of those tiny magnets are pulled in the other direction. The material itself has now become magnetic.

Applications of magnetism

Electromagnets are important components of many appliances, ranging from machines as large as particle accelerators (atom-smashers) to devices as small as pocket radios. They are used in household appliances that include dishwashers and washing machines; in electric meters; in loudspeakers, telephones, and earphones; in magnetic recording and storing devices; and in MRI (magnetic resonance imaging) devices (a diagnostic tool now found in most hospitals).

Malnutrition

Malnutrition is a condition in which a person's diet is inadequate to meet minimum daily requirements for nutrients such as proteins, fats, vitamins, and minerals. It is caused by one of two factors. First, a person simply may not get enough food to eat and, thus, fails to take in the nutrients needed to remain healthy. Someone who is hungry all the time obviously is not eating enough food to remain healthy. Second, a person may eat a limited diet that fails to deliver vital nutrients to the body. Anyone who tries to survive on a diet consisting of potato chips, candy bars, and sodas will not be getting the complete range of nutrients his or her body needs.

Individuals at risk for malnutrition

The single most important factor that leads to malnourishment is poverty. Vast numbers of people who live in less-developed countries of the world either do not get enough to eat or do not eat the correct foods. Those who are most at risk of malnutrition where conditions of poverty exist are infants, children, pregnant women, and the elderly.

Malnutrition is not restricted to less-developed nations, however. Even countries with high standards of living, such as the United States, have their share of poor people who are underfed or poorly fed and may develop malnutrition. According to some estimates, at least 20 million Americans go hungry periodically within any given month.

Throughout the world, the death toll from malnutrition caused by hunger is estimated to range from 40,000 to 50,000 people a day. An additional 450 million to 1.3 billion people face the prospect of starvation from their limited food supplies.

Elderly people in nursing homes or hospitals suffering from long-term illnesses or chronic metabolic disorders (which affect the way one's body processes food for energy) are also at risk for malnutrition. Health professionals have procedures to monitor the nutritional condition of these individuals. Malnutrition is also experienced by those suffering from a condition called anorexia nervosa, a disorder marked by a person's intentional refusal to eat properly that can lead to starvation.

Nutritional deficiency diseases

The human body requires a wide range of nutrients in order to remain healthy, grow normally, and develop properly. These nutrients in-

▼ Words to Know

Bone marrow: The spongy center of many bones in which blood cells are manufactured.

Dermatitis: An inflammation of the skin that is often a symptom of a vitamin deficiency disorder.

Edema: An abnormal collection of fluids in the body tissues.

Hemolytic anemia: A type of anemia caused by destruction of red blood cells at a rate faster than which they can be produced.

Hemorrhage: Bleeding.

Kwashiorkor: A protein-deficiency disorder found among children characterized by wasting, loss of hair and skin pigmentation, anemia, blindness, and other symptoms.

Marasmus: A protein- and calorie-deficiency disorder characterized by the wasting away of muscle and skin in children.

Night blindness: Inability to see at night often caused by a vitamin A deficiency.

Protein: Large molecules that are essential to the structure and functioning of all living cells.

clude carbohydrates, fats, proteins, vitamins, and minerals. Other substances, such as water and fiber, have no nutritional value but are needed to maintain normal body functions.

Nutrients serve a number of functions in the human body. Carbohydrates and fats, for example, are used by the body to produce the energy humans require to stay alive and healthy and to grow and develop normally. Proteins are used in the production of new body parts, to protect the body against disease and infection, in the regulation of bodily functions, and in a variety of other ways. Vitamins and minerals are used in the body for a number of different purposes, such as controlling the rate at which many chemical changes take place in the body. Overall, more than 50 different nutrients are needed to keep the human body healthy. The absence of any one of these nutrients can result in the development of a nutritional deficiency disease. Some common nutritional deficiency diseases are discussed below.

Kwashiorkor and marasmus. Kwashiorkor (from the West African word for "displaced child") is a nutritional deficiency disease caused when infants and very young children are weaned from their mother's milk and placed on a diet consisting of maize flour, cassava, or low-protein cereals. That diet is generally high in calories and carbohydrates, but low in protein. The most striking symptom of kwashiorkor is edema, a bloating caused by the accumulation of liquids under the skin. Other symptoms may include loss of hair and skin pigmentation, scaliness of the skin, and diarrhea. As the disease progresses, a person may develop anemia (a disorder in which a person's red blood cell count is low and they lack energy), digestive disorders, brain damage, a loss of appetite, irritability, and apathy (lack of interest in things).

Most children do not die of kwashiorkor directly. Instead, they develop infections that, if left untreated, can be fatal. They die from measles, the flu, diarrhea, or other conditions that could be treated relatively easily in a healthy child.

Marasmus (from the Greek word for "to waste away") is a more severe condition than kwashiorkor. It results when a person's diet is low in both calories and protein. The disease is characterized by low body weight, wasting of muscle tissue, shriveled skin, and diarrhea. The most prominent feature of marasmus is a severely bloated belly. A child with marasmus has the appearance of an old person trapped in a young person's body.

Scurvy. Scurvy is one of the oldest deficiency diseases recorded and the first one to be cured by adding a vitamin to the diet. It was a common disease among sailors during the age of exploration of the New World. Portuguese explorer Vasco da Gama (c. 1460–1524) is said to have lost half his crew to scurvy in his journey around the Cape of Good Hope at the end of the fifteenth century.

The main symptom of scurvy is hemorrhaging, the heavy discharge of blood that results when a blood vessel is broken. The gums swell and usually become infected. Wounds heal slowly and the bleeding that occurs in or around vital organs can be fatal. The disease is slow to develop and its early stages are characterized by fatigue (tiredness), irritability, and depression. In the advanced stages of the disease, laboratory tests will show an absence of the vitamin needed to protect against the disease.

In 1747, a British naval physician, James Lind (1716–1794), discovered the cause of scurvy. He found that sailors who were given oranges, lemons, and limes to eat along with their regular food did not develop scurvy. In spite of this finding, it was not until the end of the eighteenth century that the British navy finally had its sailors drink a daily portion of lime or lemon juice to prevent scurvy. The American slang term for English sailors, "limeys," originated from that practice.

The active ingredient in citrus fruits that prevents scurvy was not discovered until the 1930s. Then, two research teams, one headed by Hungarian-American biochemist Albert Szent-Györgyi (1893–1986) and the other by American biochemist Charles G. King, found that the anti-scurvy agent in citrus fruits is a compound now known as vitamin C.

Beriberi. Beriberi is a disease that occurs widely in China, Indonesia, Malaysia, Burma, India, the Philippines, and other parts of Asia and the South Pacific Ocean. It is characterized by edema (accumulation of water in body tissues), fatigue, loss of appetite, numbness or tingling in the legs, and general weakness of the body. In fact, the name beriberi comes from the Singhalese word for "weakness."

Beriberi is caused by an absence of vitamin B_1 (thiamine) in the diet. The disease can be prevented by eating foods that are rich in this vitamin, foods such as meats, wheat germ, whole grain and enriched bread, legumes (beans), peanuts, peanut butter, and nuts.

Pellagra. The symptoms of pellagra are sometimes referred to as the "three Ds": diarrhea, dermatitis, and dementia. Dermatitis refers to skin infections while dementia means deterioration of the mind. If the disease is not treated, it may lead to death. The cause for pellagra was discovered in the early twentieth century by Joseph Goldberger (1881–1929), a member of the United States Public Health Service. Goldberger established that pellagra is caused by an insufficient amount of niacin (vitamin B_3).

Niacin occurs naturally in foods such as liver, meat, fish, legumes, and dried yeast. Today it is added to many processed foods such as bread, flour, cornmeal, macaroni, and white rice. This practice has essentially eliminated pellagra as a medical problem in developed countries, although it remains a serious health problem in some less-developed countries of the world.

Rickets. Rickets is a bone disorder caused by a lack of vitamin D. Vitamin D is often called the "sunshine" vitamin because it can be produced in the human body by the effects of sunlight on the skin. Rickets was once a common disease of infants and children. However, all milk and infant formulas now have vitamin D added to them. Thus, the disorder is rarely seen today in countries where "fortified" milk is available. Symptoms of rickets include legs that have become bowed by the weight of the body and wrists and ankles that are thickened. Teeth may be badly affected and take a longer time to mature.

Other vitamin deficiency diseases.   The most common problem associated with a deficiency of vitamin A is night blindness. Night blindness is the inability to see well in the dark. Vitamin A is needed for the formation of a pigment needed by the eyes for night vision. Another eye disease caused by vitamin A deficiency is xerophthalmia, which can lead to blindness. This condition affects the cells of the cornea, other eye tissues, and the tear ducts, which stop secreting tears. Vitamin A deficiency is also responsible for a number of skin conditions, problems with tasting and smelling, and difficulties with the reproductive system.

Important sources of vitamin A that can protect against such problems include fish-liver oils, butter, egg yolks, green and yellow vegetables, and milk.

Vitamin E and K deficiencies are rare. A deficiency of vitamin E may be related to sterility (inability to have children) and to more rapid aging. Vitamin K promotes normal blood clotting.

Vitamin B_{12} (cobalamin) provides protection against pernicious anemia and mental disorders. Vitamin B_6 also protects against anemia as well as dermatitis, irritability, and convulsions.

Mineral deficiency diseases.   About 25 mineral elements are required in the human body for the maintenance of good health. Calcium and phosphorus, for example, are needed to produce teeth and bones. Diseases resulting from the lack of a mineral are relatively rare among humans. One of the exceptions is the disorder known as goiter. Goiter is a condition caused by an insufficient amount of iodine in the diet. Iodine is used by the thyroid to produce hormones that control the body's normal functioning as well as its normal growth. If sufficient iodine is not available in a person's diet, the thyroid gland begins to enlarge its cells in an effort to produce the needed hormones. This enlargement produces the characteristic swelling in the neck characteristic of goiter. Today, goiter has virtually disappeared from most developed nations because of the practice of adding small amounts of iodine (in the form of sodium iodide) to ordinary table salt.

Perhaps the most common of all mineral deficiency disorders is anemia. The term anemia literally means "a lack of blood." The condition is caused when the number of red blood cells is reduced to a level lower than that necessary for normal body functioning.

The human body gets the energy it needs to stay alive and function normally by oxidizing nutrients in cells. The oxygen needed for this process is carried from the lungs to cells on red blood cells. The "working part" of a red blood cell is a complex molecule called hemoglobin. Each hemoglobin molecule contains a single atom of iron at its center.

The iron atom combines with oxygen from the lungs to form a compound known as oxyhemoglobin. It is in this form that oxygen is transferred from the lungs to cells.

If the body fails to receive sufficient amounts of iron, an adequate number of hemoglobin molecules will not be formed. In that case, there are not enough functioning red blood cells to carry all the oxygen that cells need to produce energy. A person becomes weak and listless and may suffer headaches, soreness of the mouth, drowsiness, slight fever, gastrointestinal disturbances, and other discomforts.

A mother and child suffering from severe malnutrition at the Denunay World Vision Feeding Center in Somalia. *(Reproduced by permission of Photo Researchers, Inc.)*

More than 30 different forms of anemia have been recognized. These forms may result from a wide range of causes. For example, a person who has surgery may lose enough blood to develop anemia. A form of anemia known as aplastic anemia develops when bone marrow is destroyed by radiation, toxic chemicals, or certain types of medication. Loss of bone marrow inhibits the production of red blood cells. Hemolytic anemia is caused by the rupture of red blood cells, a problem that can be caused by hereditary factors or by toxic agents.

Treatment

The treatment for malnutrition and for nutrient deficiency diseases is obvious: a person who lacks adequate amounts of food or fails to eat the right kinds of food must change his or her diet. That instruction is easy to give but in many parts of the world it is impossible to follow. Marasmus, kwashiorkor, beriberi, scurvy, rickets, and other deficiency disorders are common in less-developed countries of the world because sufficient food is either not available or, if it is, it is not sufficiently nutritious.

In more-developed countries of the world, people often have ready access to nutritious foods in sufficient quantities so that malnutrition is less of a problem than it is in less-developed countries. In addition, a very large variety of supplements are available, such as vitamin and mineral pills. Anyone who fears that he or she may not be receiving enough of any given vitamin or mineral can easily supplement his or her diet with products available at the corner grocery store.

[*See also* **Blood; Nutrient deficiency diseases; Nutrition; Sickle-cell anemia**]

Mammals

More than 4,000 species of living mammals belong to the vertebrate class *Mammalia*. This diverse group of animals has certain common features: all have four legs, bodies covered by hair, a high and constant body temperature, a muscular diaphragm used in breathing, a lower jaw consisting of a single bone, and three bones in the middle ear. In addition, all female mammals have milk-producing glands. There are three living subclasses of mammals: the *Monotremata* (egg-laying mammals), the *Marsupialia* (pouched mammals), and the *Placentalia* (placental mammals).

Mammals range in size from bats, some of which weigh less than an ounce, to the blue whale, which weighs more than 200,000 pounds. Mammals are found in arctic climates, in hot deserts, and in every terrain in between. Marine mammals, such as whales and seals, spend most of their time in the ocean. Mammals are not as numerous and diverse as other classes of animals, such as birds or insects. Nonetheless, mammals have a tremendous impact on the environment, particularly because of the activities of one species of mammal: humans.

Adaptations

Species of mammals have developed a variety of adaptations in response to the different environments in which they live. Mammals in cold climates have insulating layers consisting of a thick coat of fur or a thick layer of fat (blubber). This layer helps retain body heat and keeps the animal's body temperature constant. Some mammals that live in deserts survive by special adaptations in their kidneys and sweat glands that allow them to survive when only very small amounts of water are available to them. Other adaptations for survival in extreme climates include hibernation (a state of winter dormancy) or estivation (summer dormancy). These responses make it possible for the animal to conserve energy when food supplies become scarce.

A grizzly bear and three cubs in Yellowstone National Park in Wyoming. The bear is considered a threatened species in the lower 48 states. *(Reproduced by permission of National Parks Service.)*

Care and development of the young

The care of the young animals is notable among mammals. Born at an average of 10 percent of its mother's weight, mammalian young grow rapidly. The protection the young receive from one or both parents during the early stages of their lives enables mammals to maintain a strong survival rate in the animal kingdom.

The subclass *Placentalia* contains the majority of living mammals. The embryo of placentals develops in the mother's uterus (womb), is nourished by blood from the placenta (an organ in the uterus), and is retained until it reaches an advanced state of development. The young of the *Marsupialia*, by contrast, develop inside the uterus of the mother, usually with a placenta connected to a yolk sac. Young marsupials are born in a very undeveloped state and are sheltered in a pouch that contains the nipples of the milk glands. Kangaroos, wallabies, and most Australian mammals are marsupials, as is the opossum of the Americas.

The *Monotremata* have hair and secrete milk like other mammals, but they lay eggs. Monotremes in Australia include the duck-billed platypus and two species of spiny anteaters.

Marijuana

Marijuana is the common name for the drug obtained from the hemp plant, *Cannabis sativa*. Hemp is a tall annual plant that can grow in almost any climate. Native to central and western Asia, hemp is one of the oldest crops cultivated by humans. Hemp's most common agricultural use has been as a source of linen, rope, canvas, and paper.

Hemp contains more than 400 chemicals. The main psychoactive (affecting the mind or behavior) chemical is tetrahydrocannabinol, commonly referred to as THC. For over 3,000 years, the dried ground leaves, flowers, and stems of the plant have been smoked, eaten, chewed, or brewed as a medicine to relieve symptoms of illness. From the seventeenth to the early twentieth century, marijuana was considered a household drug useful for treating such maladies as headaches, menstrual cramps, and toothaches.

In the 1920s, as a result of the Eighteenth Amendment to the U.S. Constitution forbidding the manufacture and sale of alcoholic beverages (Prohibition), the use of marijuana as a psychoactive drug began to grow. Even after the repeal of Prohibition in 1933, marijuana (along with mor-

Words to Know

Cannabis sativa: The botanical name for the hemp (marijuana) plant.

Dopamine: Brain chemical responsible for causing feelings of reward.

Glaucoma: An eye disease that seems to be helped by the main psychoactive compound in marijuana.

Hashish: A more potent form of marijuana that comes from the flower clusters and top leaves of the female hemp plant.

Prohibition: Eighteenth Amendment to the U.S. Constitution that prohibited the use and sale of alcohol.

Psychoactive drugs: Drugs that contain chemicals that effect the mind or behavior.

Tetrahydrocannabinol (THC): The main psychoactive compound in marijuana.

phine, heroin, and cocaine) continued to be widely used. In 1937, 46 states banned the use of marijuana.

In 1985, the Food and Drug Administration (FDA) gave approval for the use of two psychoactive chemicals from marijuana to prevent nausea and vomiting after chemotherapy in cancer treatment. Medical researchers also propose using marijuana to ease the effects of glaucoma (a serious vision disorder), as a bronchodilator (a drug that helps open the bronchial air passages in the lungs), and as an antidepressant.

The origin of the word marijuana is not known, but it appears to be a combination of the Spanish names Maria and Juana (Mary and Jane). The drug slang for marijuana includes such names as Mary Jane, pot, grass, herb, tea, reefer, and weed. Hashish is the highest grade of marijuana. It is made from the resin found on flower clusters and top leaves of the female hemp plant.

Effects

The effects of marijuana on a user change dramatically as the dosage increases. Taken at low doses, marijuana tends to make a user drowsy and relaxed. The user may also feel a general sense of well-being. As the dose increases, a user may experience an altered sense of time and awareness, and may have difficulty completing thoughts and taking part in conversation. A user's sense of balance and short-term memory (remembering very recent events or from one moment to the next) may also be affected. At higher doses, severe psychological disturbances can take place, such as paranoia, hallucinations, and panic attacks.

Marijuana affects the cardiovascular system by increasing heart rate and dilating (expanding) blood vessels in the eyes. Difficulty in coordinating body movements and pains in the chest may be other effects of the drug. Scientists believe that long-term use of marijuana damages the lungs in a manner similar to tobacco smoking.

Scientific studies released in mid-1997 indicate that people who smoke large amounts of marijuana may experience changes in their brain chemistry. These changes are similar to those seen in the brains of people who abuse addictive drugs such as heroin, cocaine, nicotine, and alcohol.

An illustration of marijuana, *Cannabis sativa.*

All addictive drugs increase the amount of dopamine in the brain. Dopamine is a brain chemical responsible for causing feelings of reward. The new studies found (for the first time) that high doses of marijuana increased the levels of dopamine in the brain. Constant use of addictive drugs, however, can cause the brain to lose its ability to produce high levels of dopamine. When this happens, a drug user feels a greater need for the drug, or for even stronger drugs. Scientists believe this may occur with marijuana.

Users of addictive drugs feel withdrawal symptoms (feeling anxious, edgy, and unable to cope) when they stop taking the drugs. It was previously believed that marijuana users did not suffer feelings of withdrawal. However, the recent studies indicate that heavy users of marijuana smoke not so much for the "high" but to calm their feelings of anxiety brought on by withdrawal from the drug. Since THC is absorbed primarily in the fat tissues and lingers in the bloodstream, withdrawal symptoms are not as evident as with fast-acting drugs like nicotine.

Possible medical benefits

In 1985, the FDA gave approval for the use of two psychoactive chemicals from marijuana to help prevent the nausea and vomiting many cancer patients experience after receiving chemotherapy. For these patients, THC can be prescribed in capsule form.

Research suggests that compounds (other than THC) inhaled when smoking marijuana can also be used for medicinal purposes. Marijuana may help stop the weight loss in AIDS patients, it may lower eye pressure in people with glaucoma, it may control spasms in multiple sclerosis patients, and it may help relieve chronic pain. Currently, thirteen states have legalized marijuana for medicinal purposes. None of these states, however, actually distribute the medicinal marijuana because it is still illegal to buy the drug from the federal government.

In mid-1999, the National Institutes of Health (NIH) issued a policy that stated the need for further research into the possible use of marijuana for medical treatment. In May 2001, the U.S. Supreme Court ruled that medical use of marijuana violates federal law and that there could be no exception.

[*See also* **Addiction**]

A dried, compressed brick of marijuana. *(Reproduced by permission of Photo Researchers, Inc.)*

Mars

Mars, the fourth planet from the Sun, was named for the Roman god of war. It is a barren, desolate, crater-covered world prone to frequent, violent dust storms. It has little oxygen, no liquid water, and ultraviolet radiation that would kill any known life-form. Temperatures range from about 80°F (27°C) at midday to about −100°F (−73°C) at midnight. Because of its striking red appearance in the sky, Mars is known as the "red planet."

Mars is roughly 140 million miles (225 million kilometers) away from the Sun. It has a diameter of 4,200 miles (6,800 kilometers), just over half the diameter of Earth. Its rotation on its axis is slightly longer than one Earth day. Since it takes Mars 687 (Earth) days to orbit the Sun, its seasons are about twice as long as those on Earth.

Physical properties of Mars

Mars has numerous Earthlike features. The two distinguishing features mark the planet's northern hemisphere. The first is a 15-mile-high (24-kilometer-high) volcano called Olympus Mons. Measuring 375 miles (600 kilometers) across, it is larger than any other in the solar system.

Mars, as seen from space by *Viking 1*. The planet is slightly more than one-tenth as massive as Earth. *(Reproduced by permission of National Aeronautics and Space Administration.)*

The second is a 2,500-mile-long (4,000-kilometer-long) canyon called Valle Marineris, eleven-and-a-half times as long and twice as deep as the Grand Canyon. The southern hemisphere is noteworthy for Hellas, an ancient canyon that was long ago filled with lava and is now a large, light area covered with dust.

Mars is also marked by what appear to be dried riverbeds and flash-flood channels. These features could mean that ice below the surface melts and is brought above ground by occasional volcanic activity. The water may temporarily flood the landscape before boiling away in the low atmospheric pressure. Another theory is that these eroded areas could be left over from a warmer, wetter period in Martian history. Mars has two polar caps. The northern one is larger and colder than the southern. Two small moons, Phobos and Deimos, orbit the planet.

Exploration of Mars

Beginning in the early 1960s, both the former Soviet Union and the United States sent unmanned spacecraft to Mars in an attempt to learn more about the planet. Although some of those missions were unsuccessful, others were able to transmit data back to Earth. In 1965, the U.S. probe *Mariner 4* flew past Mars, sending back 22 pictures of the planet's cratered surface. It also revealed that Mars has a thin atmosphere composed mostly of carbon dioxide and that the atmospheric pressure at the surface of Mars is less than 1 percent of that on Earth.

The 1969 fly-by flights of *Mariner 6* and *Mariner 7* produced 201 new images of Mars, as well as more detailed measurements of the structure and composition of its atmosphere and surface. From these measurements, scientists determined that the polar ice caps are made of haze, dry ice, and clouds.

Two years later, *Mariner 9* became the first spacecraft to orbit Mars. During its year in orbit, *Mariner 9*'s two television cameras sent back pictures of an intense Martian dust storm as well as images of 90 percent of the planet's surface and the two Martian moons. It observed an older, cratered surface on Mars's southern hemisphere and younger surface features on the northern hemisphere.

Viking **probes.**   In 1976, the United States launched the *Viking 1* and *Viking 2* space probes. Each *Viking* spacecraft consisted of both an orbiter and a lander. *Viking 1* made the first successful soft landing on Mars on July 20, 1976. A soft landing is one in which the spacecraft is intact and functional on landing. Soon after, *Viking 2* landed on the other side of the planet. Cameras from both landers showed rust-colored rocks and boulders with a reddish sky above. The rust color is due to the presence of iron oxide in the Martian soil.

The *Viking* orbiters sent back weather reports and pictures of almost the entire surface of the planet. They found that although the Martian atmosphere contains low levels of nitrogen, oxygen, carbon, and argon, it is made primarily of carbon dioxide and thus cannot support human life. The soil samples collected by the landers show no sign of past or present life on the planet.

Possible life?

In August 1996, scientists announced they had found possible traces of early Martian life in a potato-sized igneous rock. The small meteorite had been flung into space by the impact of a huge asteroid or comet 15 million years ago. It then wandered about space until it fell on the Antarctic ice sheet about 13,000 years ago. Geologists discovered the meteorite (along with more than a dozen others) in buried ice in 1984. Upon examining the rock, scientists found what they believe are fossilized remains of microorganisms that might have existed on Mars during an early part of its history when it was warmer and wetter.

New era in exploration

In 1996, the National Aeronautics and Space Administration (NASA) marked a new era in exploration when it began a ten-year campaign to explore various regions of Mars. The goal of the campaign is to discover whether life in any form ever existed—or still exists—on the red planet.

Mars Global Surveyor. The campaign began with the launch of the *Mars Global Surveyor* on November 7, 1996. The *Surveyor* established an orbit 250 miles (400 kilometers) above the surface of the planet in September 1997. The spacecraft's two-year mission was to map systematically the surface of the planet. To do so, it used a laser altimeter to map mountains and valleys; a camera system to record land forms and clouds; and detectors to measure atmospheric composition, radiation, and surface minerals.

The *Surveyor*'s first major discovery was to solve one of the greatest mysteries surrounding Mars: the planet does possess a magnetic field. A magnetic field is usually generated by molten metal at a planet's core. On the surface, the field shields a planet and life on it from cosmic and solar radiation. Although Mars's field is weak, its existence adds evidence to the possibility that life may have existed on the planet long ago.

In April 1999, the *Surveyor* sent back to Earth some astonishing information: the crust of Mars's surface has alternating layers of magnetic fields. Scientists theorize that the magnetic bands are formed when magma from far below the surface of Mars is forced to the surface by plate tectonics. (Plate tectonics is a geological theory that Earth's surface is composed of rigid plates or sections that move about the surface in response to internal pressure.) As the magma cools and hardens into a new layer of crust, the iron in the magma is magnetized towards the current magnetic field. This discovery could point to a past of geologic activity similar to that of the Earth and possibly very early on in its history supported simple life forms.

In June 2000, scientists studying pictures sent back by *Surveyor* announced that the standard description of Mars as cold, desolate, and dry would have to be changed. The pictures clearly showed channels and grooves on the steep, inside walls of craters that indicate the downward flow of water. These surface features appear to be evidence of water in the upper crust of Mars that had seeped through and run down the channels. Scientists suggested that these water flows happened in recent geological time—perhaps just a few hundreds, thousands, or millions of years ago.

In December 2000, after further analysis of pictures sent back by *Surveyor,* scientists announced that in its earlier history, Mars was a

A photograph of the Martian surface taken by one of the *Viking* landers. The layer of morning frost that can be seen in the photo is less than one-thousandth of an inch thick. *(Reproduced by permission of National Aeronautics and Space Administration.)*

warmer world with a denser atmosphere, and its surface was covered with lakes and shallow seas. They based these assumptions on evidence of distinct, thick layers of rock within craters and other depressions on the surface of the planet.

After having gathered tens of thousands of images of Mars, the *Mars Global Surveyor* completed its mapping mission in early 2001. Its main mission accomplished, the probe was given additional scientific work to complete, including scouting out landing sites for future spacecraft. NASA engineers hope to use *Surveyor* to relay commands to twin rovers slated to land on the planet in early 2004.

Mars Pathfinder and the Sojourner rover. On December 4, 1996, less than a month after the launch of the *Mars Global Surveyor,* NASA launched the *Mars Pathfinder.* Six months later, on July 4, 1997, the *Mars Pathfinder* landed successfully on Mars in the plain of Ares Vallis and released the Sojourner rover.

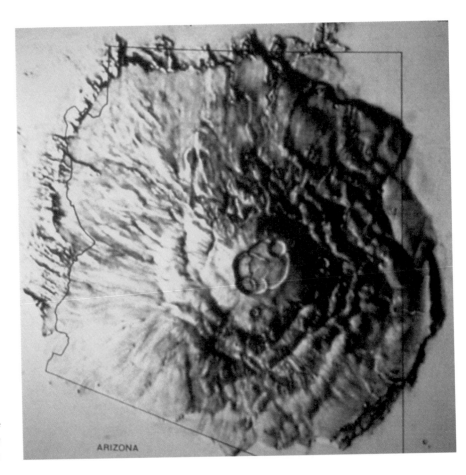

The largest volcano on Mars, Olympus Mons, is much larger than the largest volcano on Earth. Olympus Mons is over 15.5 miles (25 kilometers) tall—three times as much as Mount Everest—and has a base the size of Arizona. This photo shows how large Olympus Mons is compared to Arizona. *(Reproduced by permission of National Aeronautics and Space Administration.)*

ARIZONA

From pictures sent back by the *Mars Pathfinder,* scientists deduced the plain where the spacecraft landed had once been reshaped by colossal floods. The tilt of rocks and the tails of debris behind pebbles in the area led scientists to estimate that the main flood was hundreds of miles wide, hundreds of feet deep, and flowed for thousands of miles. Scientists could not answer the question of where the water went.

Part of the mission of the rover was to record the chemical makeup of rocks and the soil. The instruments on Sojourner revealed that Mars has a history of repeated cycles of internal melting, cooling, and remelting. The rocks analyzed contained large amounts of the mineral quartz, which is produced when the material is melted and remelted many times. Sojourner's examination also revealed that Mars seems much more like Earth geologically than the Moon does. The Martian rocks analyzed resemble a common Earth volcanic rock named andesite.

These findings support scientific theories that Mars has been convulsed (literally turned inside out) by internal heat through much of its 4.6-billion-year history.

Lost missions.   In 1999, NASA suffered a double blow when two spacecraft, each on a mission to Mars, were lost. In September of that year, the *Mars Climate Orbiter* was to have reached Mars, settled into an orbit, explored the Martian atmosphere, and acted as a communications relay station. However, because technicians failed to convert metric and English measurements in navigational instructions sent to the spacecraft, it flew in too close to the planet and most likely burned in the atmosphere before crashing. It was never heard from again. Just three months later, in December, the *Mars Polar Lander* was scheduled to have landed on Mars to begin prospecting the landscape of dirt and ice for traces of water and evidence of the planet's climatic history. However, scientists for the project never heard from the 1,200-pound (545-kilogram) robotic spacecraft after it was supposed to have landed. They speculate that a software glitch in the spacecraft's program caused it to crash just moments before its projected landing.

Future expeditions.   In October 2000, NASA unveiled an ambitious plan to send eight or more probes to Mars over the next two decades to search for evidence of water or life. The first of these, *Mars Odyssey,* was launched in the spring of 2001, with a planned arrival in the fall. Once in orbit, the spacecraft will try to determine the composition of the planet's surface, to detect water and shallow buried ice, and to study the radiation environment. In mid-2003, in a mission planned by the European Space Agency and the Italian Space Agency, NASA will launch the

Mars Express. This spacecraft's main mission will be to search for subsurface water from orbit and to deliver a lander to the Martian surface. That lander, the *Beagle 2*, will sniff air, dig dirt, and bake rock samples for evidence of past or present life.

Also in 2003, NASA will send two powerful rovers to Mars that will be identical to each other, but will land at different regions of the planet. These robotic explorers will be able to trek up to 328 feet (100 meters) across the Martian surface each day in search of evidence of liquid water that may have been present in the planet's past.

In 2005, NASA plans to launch a powerful scientific orbiter, the *Mars Reconnaissance Orbiter.* The orbiter will map the Martian surface with an eagle-eyed camera, trying to bridge the gap between surface observations and measurements taken from orbit. The camera will have an unprecedented 8-inch (20-centimeter) resolution, allowing it to record features as small as a license plate. In 2007, NASA plans to launch a roving long-range, long-duration science laboratory that will provide extensive surface measurements and pave the way for a future sample return mission.

[*See also* **Solar system**]

Where to Learn More

Books

Earth Sciences

Cox, Reg, and Neil Morris. *The Natural World.* Philadelphia, PA: Chelsea House, 2000.

Dasch, E. Julius, editor. *Earth Sciences for Students.* Four volumes. New York: Macmillan Reference, 1999.

Denecke, Edward J., Jr. *Let's Review: Earth Science.* Second edition. Hauppauge, NY: Barron's, 2001.

Engelbert, Phillis. *Dangerous Planet: The Science of Natural Disasters.* Three volumes. Farmington Hills, MI: UXL, 2001.

Gardner, Robert. *Human Evolution.* New York: Franklin Watts, 1999.

Hall, Stephen. *Exploring the Oceans.* Milwaukee, WI: Gareth Stevens, 2000.

Knapp, Brian. *Earth Science: Discovering the Secrets of the Earth.* Eight volumes. Danbury, CT: Grolier Educational, 2000.

Llewellyn, Claire. *Our Planet Earth.* New York: Scholastic Reference, 1997.

Moloney, Norah. *The Young Oxford Book of Archaeology.* New York: Oxford University Press, 1997.

Nardo, Don. *Origin of Species: Darwin's Theory of Evolution.* San Diego, CA: Lucent Books, 2001.

Silverstein, Alvin, Virginia Silverstein, and Laura Silverstein Nunn. *Weather and Climate.* Brookfield, CN: Twenty-First Century Books, 1998.

Williams, Bob, Bob Ashley, Larry Underwood, and Jack Herschbach. *Geography.* Parsippany, NJ: Dale Seymour Publications, 1997.

Life Sciences

Barrett, Paul M. *National Geographic Dinosaurs.* Washington, D.C.: National Geographic Society, 2001.

Fullick, Ann. *The Living World.* Des Plaines, IL: Heinemann Library, 1999.

Gamlin, Linda. *Eyewitness: Evolution.* New York: Dorling Kindersley, 2000.

Greenaway, Theresa. *The Plant Kingdom: A Guide to Plant Classification and Biodiversity.* Austin, TX: Raintree Steck-Vaughn, 2000.

Kidd, J. S., and Renee A Kidd. *Life Lines: The Story of the New Genetics.* New York: Facts on File, 1999.

Kinney, Karin, editor. *Our Environment.* Alexandria, VA: Time-Life Books, 2000.

Nagel, Rob. *Body by Design: From the Digestive System to the Skeleton.* Two volumes. Farmington Hills, MI: UXL., 2000.

Parker, Steve. *The Beginner's Guide to Animal Autopsy: A "Hands-in" Approach to Zoology, the World of Creatures and What's Inside Them.* Brookfield, CN: Copper Beech Books, 1997.

Pringle, Laurence. *Global Warming: The Threat of Earth's Changing Climate.* New York: SeaStar Books, 2001.

Riley, Peter. *Plant Life.* New York: Franklin Watts, 1999.

Stanley, Debbie. *Genetic Engineering: The Cloning Debate.* New York: Rosen Publishing Group, 2000.

Whyman, Kate. *The Animal Kingdom: A Guide to Vertebrate Classification and Biodiversity.* Austin, TX: Raintree Steck-Vaughn, 1999.

Physical Sciences

Allen, Jerry, and Georgiana Allen. *The Horse and the Iron Ball: A Journey Through Time, Space, and Technology.* Minneapolis, MN: Lerner Publications, 2000.

Berger, Samantha, *Light.* New York: Scholastic, 1999.

Bonnet, Bob L., and Dan Keen. *Physics.* New York: Sterling Publishing, 1999.

Clark, Stuart. *Discovering the Universe.* Milwaukee, WI: Gareth Stevens, 2000.

Fleisher, Paul, and Tim Seeley. *Matter and Energy: Basic Principles of Matter and Thermodynamics.* Minneapolis, MN: Lerner Publishing, 2001.

Gribbin, John. *Eyewitness: Time and Space.* New York: Dorling Kindersley, 2000.

Holland, Simon. *Space.* New York: Dorling Kindersley, 2001.

Kidd, J. S., and Renee A. Kidd. *Quarks and Sparks: The Story of Nuclear Power.* New York: Facts on File, 1999.

Levine, Shar, and Leslie Johnstone. *The Science of Sound and Music.* New York: Sterling Publishing, 2000

Naeye, Robert. *Signals from Space: The Chandra X-ray Observatory.* Austin, TX: Raintree Steck-Vaughn, 2001.

Newmark, Ann. *Chemistry.* New York: Dorling Kindersley, 1999.

Oxlade, Chris. *Acids and Bases.* Chicago, IL: Heinemann Library, 2001.

Vogt, Gregory L. *Deep Space Astronomy.* Brookfield, CT: Twenty-First Century Books, 1999.

Technology and Engineering Sciences

Baker, Christopher W. *Scientific Visualization: The New Eyes of Science.* Brookfield, CT: Millbrook Press, 2000.

Cobb, Allan B. *Scientifically Engineered Foods: The Debate over What's on Your Plate.* New York: Rosen Publishing Group, 2000.

Cole, Michael D. *Space Launch Disaster: When Liftoff Goes Wrong.* Springfield, NJ: Enslow, 2000.

Deedrick, Tami. *The Internet.* Austin, TX: Raintree Steck-Vaughn, 2001.

DuTemple, Leslie A. *Oil Spills.* San Diego, CA: Lucent Books, 1999.

Gaines, Ann Graham. *Satellite Communication.* Mankata, MN: Smart Apple Media, 2000.

Gardner, Robert, and Dennis Shortelle. *From Talking Drums to the Internet: An Encyclopedia of Communications Technology.* Santa Barbara, CA: ABC-Clio, 1997.

Graham, Ian S. *Radio and Television.* Austin, TX: Raintree Steck-Vaughn, 2000.

Parker, Steve. *Lasers: Now and into the Future.* Englewood Cliffs, NJ: Silver Burdett Press, 1998.

Sachs, Jessica Snyder. *The Encyclopedia of Inventions.* New York: Franklin Watts, 2001.

Wilkinson, Philip. *Building.* New York: Dorling Kindersley, 2000.

Wilson, Anthony. *Communications: How the Future Began.* New York: Larousse Kingfisher Chambers, 1999.

Periodicals

Archaeology. Published by Archaeological Institute of America, 656 Beacon Street, 4th Floor, Boston, Massachusetts 02215. Also online at www.archaeology.org.

Astronomy. Published by Kalmbach Publishing Company, 21027 Crossroads Circle, Brookfield, WI 53186. Also online at www.astronomy.com.

Discover. Published by Walt Disney Magazine, Publishing Group, 500 S. Buena Vista, Burbank, CA 91521. Also online at www.discover.com.

National Geographic. Published by National Geographic Society, 17th & M Streets, NW, Washington, DC 20036. Also online at www.nationalgeographic.com.

New Scientist. Published by New Scientist, 151 Wardour St., London, England W1F 8WE. Also online at www.newscientist.com (includes links to more than 1,600 science sites).

Popular Science. Published by Times Mirror Magazines, Inc., 2 Park Ave., New York, NY 10024. Also online at www.popsci.com.

Science. Published by American Association for the Advancement of Science, 1333 H Street, NW, Washington, DC 20005. Also online at www.sciencemag.org.

Science News. Published by Science Service, Inc., 1719 N Street, NW, Washington, DC 20036. Also online at www.sciencenews.org.

Scientific American. Published by Scientific American, Inc., 415 Madison Ave, New York, NY 10017. Also online at www.sciam.com.

Smithsonian. Published by Smithsonian Institution, Arts & Industries Bldg., 900 Jefferson Dr., Washington, DC 20560. Also online at www.smithsonianmag.com.

Weatherwise. Published by Heldref Publications, 1319 Eighteenth St., NW, Washington, DC 20036. Also online at www.weatherwise.org.

Web Sites

Cyber Anatomy (provides detailed information on eleven body systems and the special senses) *http://library.thinkquest.org/11965/*

The DNA Learning Center (provides in-depth information about genes for students and educators) *http://vector.cshl.org/*

Educational Hotlists at the Franklin Institute (provides extensive links and other resources on science subjects ranging from animals to wind energy) *http://sln.fi.edu/tfi/hotlists/hotlists.html*

ENC Web Links: Science (provides an extensive list of links to sites covering subject areas under earth and space science, physical science, life science, process skills, and the history of science) *http://www.enc.org/weblinks/science/*

ENC Web Links: Math topics (provides an extensive list of links to sites covering subject areas under topics such as advanced mathematics, algebra, geometry, data analysis and probability, applied mathematics, numbers and operations, measurement, and problem solving) *http://www.enc.org/weblinks/math/*

Encyclopaedia Britannica Discovering Dinosaurs Activity Guide *http://dinosaurs.eb.com/dinosaurs/study/*

The Exploratorium: The Museum of Science, Art, and Human Perception *http://www.exploratorium.edu/*

ExploreMath.com (provides highly inter-active math activities for students and ed-ucators) *http://www.exploremath.com/*

ExploreScience.com (provides highly in-teractive science activities for students and educators) *http://www.explorescience.com/*

Imagine the Universe! (provides informa-tion about the universe for students aged 14 and up) *http://imagine.gsfc.nasa.gov/*

Mad Sci Network (highly searchable site provides extensive science information in addition to a search engine and a library to find science resources on the Internet; also allows students to submit questions to sci-entists) *http://www.madsci.org/*

The Math Forum (provides math-related information and resources for elementary through graduate-level students) *http://forum.swarthmore.edu/*

NASA Human Spaceflight: International Space Station (NASA homepage for the space station) *http://www.spaceflight.nasa.gov/station/*

NASA's Origins Program (provides up-to-the-minute information on the scientific quest to understand life and its place in the universe) *http://origins.jpl.nasa.gov/*

National Human Genome Research Insti-tute (provides extensive information about the Human Genome Project) *http://www.nhgri.nih.gov:80/index.html*

New Scientist Online Magazine *http://www.newscientist.com/*

The Nine Planets (provides a multimedia tour of the history, mythology, and current scientific knowledge of each of the planets and moons in our solar system) *http://seds.lpl.arizona.edu/nineplanets/nineplanets/nineplanets.html*

The Particle Adventure (provides an in-teractive tour of quarks, neutrinos, anti-matter, extra dimensions, dark matter, ac-celerators, and particle detectors) *http://particleadventure.org/*

PhysLink: Physics and astronomy online ed-ucation and reference *http://physlink.com/*

Savage Earth Online (online version of the PBS series exploring earthquakes, volca-noes, tsunamis, and other seismic activity) *http://www.pbs.org/wnet/savageearth/*

Science at NASA (provides breaking in-formation on astronomy, space science, earth science, and biological and physical sciences) *http://science.msfc.nasa.gov/*

Science Learning Network (provides Inter-net-guided science applications as well as many middle school science links) *http://www.sln.org/*

SciTech Daily Review (provides breaking science news and links to dozens of science and technology publications; also provides links to numerous "interesting" science sites) *http://www.scitechdaily.com/*

Space.com (space news, games, entertain-ment, and science fiction) *http://www.space.com/index.html*

SpaceDaily.com (provides latest news about space and space travel) *http://www.spacedaily.com/*

SpaceWeather.com (science news and in-formation about the Sun-Earth environ-ment) *http://www.spaceweather.com/*

The Why Files (exploration of the science behind the news; funded by the National Science Foundation) *http://whyfiles.org/*

Index

Italic type indicates volume numbers; **boldface** type indicates entries and their page numbers; (ill.) indicates illustrations.

A

Abacus   *1:* **1-2** 1 (ill.)
Abelson, Philip   *1:* 24
Abortion   *3:* 565
Abrasives   *1:* **2-4,** 3 (ill.)
Absolute dating   *4:* 616
Absolute zero   *3:* 595-596
Abyssal plains   *7:* 1411
Acceleration   *1:* **4-6**
Acetylsalicylic acid   *1:* **6-9,** 8 (ill.)
Acheson, Edward G.   *1:* 2
Acid rain   *1:* **9-14,** 10 (ill.), 12 (ill.), *6:* 1163, *8:* 1553
Acidifying agents   *1:* 66
Acids and bases   *1:* **14-16,** *8:* 1495
Acoustics   *1:* **17-23,** 17 (ill.), 20 (ill.)
Acquired immunodeficiency syndrome. *See* **AIDS (acquired immunodeficiency syndrome)**
Acrophobia   *8:* 1497
Actinides   *1:* **23-26,** 24 (ill.)
Acupressure   *1:* 121
Acupuncture   *1:* 121
Adams, John Couch   *7:* 1330
Adaptation   *1:* **26-32,** 29 (ill.), 30 (ill.)
Addiction   *1:* **32-37,** 35 (ill.), *3:* 478
Addison's disease   *5:* 801

Adena burial mounds   *7:* 1300
Adenosine triphosphate   *7:* 1258
ADHD   *2:* 237-238
Adhesives   *1:* **37-39,** 38 (ill.)
Adiabatic demagnetization   *3:* 597
ADP   *7:* 1258
Adrenal glands   *5:* 796 (ill.)
Adrenaline   *5:* 800
Aerobic respiration   *9:* 1673
Aerodynamics   *1:* **39-43,** 40 (ill.)
Aerosols   *1:* **43-49,** 43 (ill.)
Africa   *1:* **49-54,** 50 (ill.), 53 (ill.)
Afterburners   *6:* 1146
Agent Orange   *1:* **54-59,** 57 (ill.)
Aging and death   *1:* **59-62**
Agoraphobia   *8:* 1497
Agriculture   *1:* **62-65,** 63, 64 (ill.), *3:*582-590, *5:* 902-903, *9:* 1743-744, *7:* 1433 (ill.)
Agrochemicals   *1:* **65-69,** 67 (ill.), 68 (ill.)
Agroecosystems   *2:* 302
AI.   *See* **Artificial intelligence**
AIDS (acquired immunodeficiency syndrome)   *1:* **70-74,** 72 (ill.), *8:* 1583, *9:* 1737
Air flow   *1:* 40 (ill.)
Air masses and fronts   *1:* **80-82,** 80 (ill.)
Air pollution   *8:* 1552, 1558
Aircraft   *1:* **74-79,** 75 (ill.), 78 (ill.)
Airfoil   *1:* 41
Airplanes.   *See* **Aircraft**
Airships   *1:* 75

H

M

O

W

X

Y